The City of York Companion

By the same authors

The City Companion

The City of York Companion

Martin Mason
Malcolm Sanders

ROBERT HALE · LONDON

Robert Hale Limited
Clerkenwell House
Clerkenwell Green
London EC1 R OHT

Printed in Great Britain by
St. Edmundsbury Press Limited,
Bury St Edmunds, Suffolk.
Bound by WBC Bookbinders Limited.

In Memoriam

Michael Floyd DFC

Contents

York Chronology

71	The 9th Legion under the command of Petilius Cerialis establishes a base at York.
98 – 117	The timber fortress is rebuilt in stone during the reign of the Emperor Trajan.
122	The Emperor Hadrian visits Britain; the 9th Legion is replaced by the 6th
211	After successful campaigns led by the Emperor Septimius Severus. Eboracum becomes the capital of 'Britannia Inferior'. Septimius dies in Eboracum, and his son, Caracalla promotes the town to the status of a 'colonia'.
306	The Emperor Constantius I Chlorus dies in Eboracum and is succeeded by his son, Constantine I, known as the Great.
395 – 455	The Romans withdraw from Britain.
c.425	The beginning of the Anglo-Saxon period.
625	St Paulinus arrives in York to re-establish Christianity: the beginning of York's pre-eminence as the religious centre of the north.
866	The Viking 'Great Army' captures York.
876-954	York is ruled by a succession of Scandinavian and English kings until Eric Bloodaxe, the last Viking king, is expelled.
1013-1042	After the conquests of Sweyn Forkbeard, all of England comes under Danish rule.

1066	The year of invasions. Harold Hardrada captures York but is defeated and killed at Stamford Bridge by Harold II. The Norman invasion under Duke William leads to the defeat and death of Harold II at Hastings.
1068-9	The Normans build castles at York.
1071	Work begins on what will become York Minster.
1088	St Mary's Abbey founded.
1137	Much of York is destroyed by fire.
1190	Massacre of Jews in Clifford's Tower.
1244	York Castle is rebuilt in stone in the reign of Henry II.
1246-1337	York becomes the temporary capital of England during the Scottish wars.
1356	Work begins on Merchant Adventurers' Hall.
1453-85	The Wars of the Roses.
1460	After his defeat at Wakefield the Duke of York's head is displayed on Micklegate Bar.
1536-39	The dissolution of all monasteries and friaries in York.
1586	The martyrdom of St Margaret Clitherow (canonized in 1970)
1642-6	The Civil War.
1644	York is besieged by Parliamentary forces and surrenders after the defeat of the Royalist Army at Marston Moor.

1730	Construction of the Mansion House, the first of its type in the country.
1739	Dick Turpin hanged at Tyburn (York Castle).
1746	The heads of some leading Jacobites are displayed on Micklegate Bar following the defeat of the '45.
1776	Terry and Sons confectionary business is established in St Helen's Square.
1784	Big improvements are made in York's water supply.
1812	The present Ouse Bridge is completed.
1823	The York Gas Light Company is established.
1835-40	Parliament Street is created.
1839	York is linked by railway to the West Riding.
1862	Tukes cocoa and chocolate business is transferred to Henry Rowntree.
1863	Lendal Bridge is completed.
1881	Skeldergate Bridge is opened.
1900	Foss Island Electricity Generating works are opened.
1966	The original railway station of 1841 is demolished.
1984	Lightning strikes York Minster.

List of Illustrations

Summary of Areas

Area A · St Mary's Abbey

Lendal Bridge · Lendal Tower · The Abbey Grounds · King's Manor ·

Area B · The Minster

High Petergate · St William's College · The Minster · Treasurer's House · Gray's Court ·

Area C · Goodramgate

Merchant Taylors' Hall · Bedern · Bartle Garth · Goodramgate · Low Petergate

Area D · Stonegate

Duncombe Place · Stonegate · Coffee Yard · Little Stonegate · Church of St Helen · Low Petergate

Area E · Lendal

St Helen's Square · The Mansion House · The Guildhall · The Judge's Lodging · The Yorkshire Club · The Assembly Rooms · St Martin, Coney Street · Richard III

Area F · Ousegate

Judge's Court · Low and High Ousegate · St William · All Saints, Pavement

Area G · The Shambles

Parliament Street · St Sampson's Square · Patrick Pool · The Shambles · St Margaret Clitherow · Colliergate

Area H · St Saviourgate

St Andrew's Hall · St Anthony's Hall · Peasholme Green · St Saviourgate · Lady Hewley

Area I · Walmgate

River Foss · Rowntree Wharf · Fossgate · Herbert House · Lady Peckett's Yard · Bowes Morrell House · Walmgate Bar · Dick Turpin · Fishergate Tower

Area J · Clifford's Tower

Castle Museum · Clifford's Tower · Fairfax House · Jorvik Viking Centre · The Davy Tower · Franciscan Friary

Area K · Skeldergate

Skeldergate Bridge · The Old Baile · Skeldergate · Bishopshill House · Lady Anne Middleton's Hotel

Area L · Micklegate

Bishopshill Junior · Micklegate · Jacob's Well · George Hudson · All Saints, North Street · Old Railway Station site · Barker Tower

Introduction
Many books have been written about the old walled city of York in all its aspects, but we are hoping that there is room for yet one more. As with our previous publication on the City of London, this book focuses primarily on the architectural side as befits our building background. It does not purport to be a work of scholarship (for true connoisseurs, the Royal Commission on Historical Monuments Inventory remains the definitive work), but rather the product of two amateur enthusiasts indulging their hobby by spending many enjoyable days wandering the streets, drinking in the atmosphere, and a few ales besides. In general we have eschewed architectural jargon, so if the occasional quoin or voussoir has crept into the text, we hope that you will forgive us.

York has been lucky, it has not suffered the periodic destructions by war, natural disaster, or redevelopment that have been the lot of the City of London. Its architectural history has been one of a gentle ebb and flow, with each succeeding period leaving its mark but not at the expense of those that have gone before. Most importantly it has been spared the crass and brutal ministrations of the town planner and road engineer that have ripped out the hearts of all too many historic British towns.

The first to recognize the strategic importance of the site were the Romans, and their creation, Eboracum, was the northernmost city of their empire and a vital military base. Many eminent Romans passed this way: Hadrian, Agricola, Septimius Severus, Constantius Chlorus and his son Constantine the Great. Most of what remains of their presence is below ground now, including the ghosts of the VI Legion, who allegedly still march through the cellars of the Treasury. Also below ground are the relics of Jorvik, the Viking trading centre that was the basis of the city that we see today.

It was with the coming of the Normans that York became what it was to remain until the industrial revolution, the 'Capital of the North' and second city of England.

With their usual passion for fortification they wasted no time in throwing up two motte-and-bailey castles either side of the Ouse, one of which grew into an impressive defensive complex. Their real legacy however, lies in the ecclesiastical field, with many of York's churches tracing their origins to the 11th and 12th centuries.

After its colourful and violent beginnings, York settled down to the serious business of making money, and the many fine medieval buildings that grace its streets are monuments to the comfortable prosperity that ensued. To many, these buildings epitomise York and provide the abiding image of the city. Less celebrated, but equally noteworthy, are the numerous elegant Baroque and Georgian buildings of the 17th and 18th centuries, a period of continuing peace and prosperity broken only briefly by the siege of 1644.

Unlike the majority of northern towns, which mushroomed in the 19th century, York, being a long-established city, has comparatively few examples of Victorian buildings in the central area. Those that do exist, however, are worthy specimens and reflect the spirit of that age which saw York become the railway capital of England.

As mentioned previously, York has experienced relatively little in the way of modern development and consequently presents a picture of delightful unity, the various periods of building existing in perfect visual harmony.

Most cities are best explored on foot. In York, thankfully, there is no other way, and with its winding streets, intriguing 'snickelways', and the icing on the cake of the city walls, it is a pedestrian's paradise. To aid the thirsty walker we have listed the many excellent watering-holes that have been so thoughtfully provided.

We hope that you will enjoy your tour of York, and that those resident north of Watford will forgive the temerity of two native Londoners writing about a city not their own.

Area A

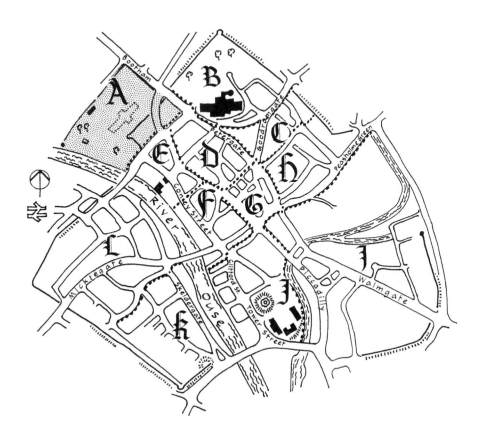

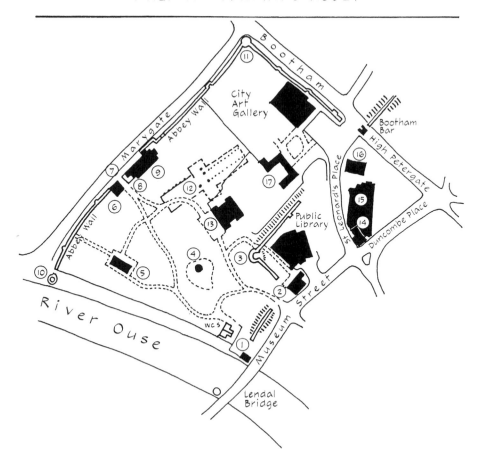

1 Lendal Tower
2 St Leonard's Hospital
3 The Multangular Tower
4 The Observatory
5 Hospitium
6 St Mary's Lodge
7 St Mary's Abbey Gatehouse
8 St Mary's Chapel
9 St Olave

10 The Water Tower
11 St Mary's Tower
12 Ruins of St Mary's Abbey
13 The Yorkshire Museum
14 The Red House
15 The Theatre Royal
16 De Grey Rooms and
   Tourist Information
17 The King's Manor

Although most of the first area to be explored does in fact lie outside the original Roman and medieval fortified City of York, the land occupied by the Benedictine Abbey of St Mary still retains large sections of its own defensive walls and towers.

If perhaps you have come from the station, our route to the Abbey starts by crossing the Lendal Bridge, which, incidentally, was opened on the 8th January 1863 and designed by Thomas Page. This must have been a busy period in his life, as Westminster Bridge had been opened the year before. In the case of Westminster, his bridge had replaced the original, built between 1738-1749. The Lendal Bridge, though, didn't replace an original, just a ferry that had operated from St Leonard's Landing for many hundreds of years. In fact, the only direct access across the river before 1863 had been the Ouse Bridge, approached from Micklegate. Skeldergate Bridge, to be mentioned in Area K, was opened in 1881.

On the left, adjacent to the bridge, is the Lendal Tower, originating from about 1300. It started life as a round tower, rather like its counterpart the Barker Tower, which can be seen on the South side of the river. In the 17th and 18th centuries the Lendal Tower was added to in both bulk and height; in the 1670s, it was used for pumping a water supply to the city from the Ouse, the water-wheels being horse-powered; in the 1750s the horses gave way to a Newcomen steam engine, and in 1784 the Newcomen engine was altered to improve its efficiency by John Smeaton (1724-1792) with a design that was built to last. Smeaton started his career by studying law, but by the 1750s his childhood bent for engineering took over. Although a designer of bridges, canals and engines, his most famous work was the Eddystone lighthouse, completed in October 1759. This was far more durable than its two rather fleeting predecessors, and lasted until 1877. John Smeaton was also a proprietor of the York Waterworks. But now, back to the Lendal Tower. The original wooden water-supply pipes were replaced with cast-iron ones in the early 19th century. The wooden system was subject to frequent blocking by sediment from unfiltered water. Fancy a glass?

In 1846 the Smeaton/Newcomen steam engine vanished, together with the associated paraphernalia and holding tank. The Tower was then lowered by ten feet, acquired the requisite castellated parapet and took on the appearance we see today. It is still, however, associated with the waterworks, having been leased for that purpose for 500 years at an annual rent of one peppercorn. That was in 1677. It now houses the York Waterworks PLC boardrooms. As a matter of interest, figures for the number of appliances served by the York New Waterworks Company are as follows: in 1850, 684 WCS and 20 baths (water supplied to 5,861 homes); by 1936 these figures had risen to 29,189 WCS and 15,712 baths (water supplied to 30,129 homes).

So, having crossed the bridge and passed the aforementioned structure, we now see a section of ancient wall of medieval origin on our left. This leads towards the remnants of St Leonard's Hospital. I see that we have just passed the entrance to the Abbey grounds. Never mind, we will return there in a minute after a quick word about the hospital. It was rebuilt in the early 13th century and paid for by a certain John Romanus (died 1255). That which we see today, part of the infirmary, is only a small part of this particular building. There had been a previous hospital on the site, founded before the Norman Conquest and known as St Peter's. However, it was King Stephen (1135–1154) who renamed it St Leonard's. In medieval times it became the largest hospital in the north of England. It was 'dissolved' in 1540, so we are lucky to have at least a glimpse of what remains.

But now to the Abbey grounds. Heading along the path, we see, on our right, the Multangular Tower. This is a partial remnant of the Roman fortress that originally encompassed the heart of the City centre. The Tower was probably built by order of the Roman Emperor Constantine I, who ruled between 308 and 337. His father, Constantius I Chlorus had come to Britain to put down a 'take-over' to Roman rule (hence the probability that the City defences were strengthened soon afterwards). Looking at the tower now, the top third or so was added in the 13th century, which coincides with the building of the medieval wall around the City.

The section of wall linked to the tower and continuing behind the public library was excavated in the 1960s. This was quite a discovery, as what was revealed was a complete section of the original Roman wall.

We can now swing to the left and cut across the grass to visit the Observatory. This was built between 1832-33 by the Yorkshire Philosophical Society, and incorporated a revolving roof previously designed by John Smeaton. It was originally designed to house instruments given to the Society by Dr Pearson, rector of South Kilworth in Leicestershire. This structure would no doubt have been of great interest to that great optician Thomas Cooke (1807-1868), a native of York, who specialized in the development of telescopes. His crowning achievement was a telescope incorporating a 25-inch object glass and 7-inch transit instrument, almost completed at the time of his death and installed at Gateshead: not bad for someone whose enthusiasm for optics was fired by grinding lenses made from the bottoms of salvaged drinking glasses. He was elected a member of the Royal Astronomical Society in 1859. The Observatory itself is both quaint and functional, but by today's standards appears small for such an important function. As the tablet on the building mentions, it was restored and refitted to mark the British Association's 150th anniversary meeting in York in 1981 and was opened by its President, HRH the Duke of Kent.

We now carry on down the grassy slope to have a look at the medieval Hospitium building. Judging by the name, this must have been a place where guests or strangers staying at the Abbey could be lodged. The building has been so well spruced up that some of the charm of such an ancient structure seems to have got lost somewhere. The lower storey is of 14th-century origin, with the upper storey built a century later. The roof was reconstructed in the 1930s, and, fortunately, in recent years the windows in the pitch of the roof, which somewhat resembled a modern attic conversion, have now been removed. The remains of the gateway to the hospice do have a more romantic crumbling look about them.

The Multangular Tower

Our next port of call is St Mary's Lodge, which flanks what was the Abbey Gatehouse. The wall we walk past to our left on the way out of the grounds via the gate, is mainly 12th century (the lower part that is; the rest of the building is 15th century, but with a new stone parapet added in 1840). On our right, and the counterpart to the wall on the left, is the remnant of the other, very attractive, Norman wall that enclosed the gatehouse. This wall has been incorporated into St Mary's Chapel, which in itself forms a part of the parish church of St Olave Marygate. The church was originally built in the 15th century on the site of a previous church that was built between 1030 and 1055. Parts of the 15th-century church remain, namely the tower, but most is 18th-century or later.

This particular corner has great historical importance in relation to the Abbey grounds as a whole. Monks from the Saxon monastery at Lastingham in the North Yorkshire Moors (founded in 654 by St Cedd), together with monks from Whitby Abbey (founded in 657 by Oswy) were given the church of St Olave after the Norman Conquest. The gift was made by Alan, Count of Brittany and Earl of Richmond, who came to England at the time of the Conquest. These Benedictine monks (followers of the creed of St Benedict who lived between c. 480 and c. 547) ensured that each monastery was autonomous, and in them prayer, study, and manual labour formed a daily routine. They were favoured by both William I (1066-1087) and William II (1087-1100), and the generous gifts these monarchs made were sufficient for the monks to start the building of what was finally to become a far grander structure, namely of course St Mary's Abbey. All the while William I was 'harrying the North' between 1069-1070 to put down mercilessly the last concerted rebellion against his rule. Alas, most of the Abbey has gone. But, strangely enough, some of the material from the ruins was used in the 18th century to carry out rebuilding works to St Olave. So one could say that matters had come full circle.

We can now go out into Marygate and walk down to the river to take a look at the Water Tower. On our left as we walk towards it is the 14th-century Abbey boundary wall; the archway adjacent to the tower was added in the early 19th century.

St Mary's Gatehouse

The wall was breached at this point so that the riverside walk could be extended through the Abbey grounds. The Tower is the same age as the wall, but was originally higher and incorporated a crenellated parapet. It was, of course, designed for defensive purposes, the walls being five feet thick and equipped with arrow-slits.

At the other end of Marygate, on the corner with Bootham, is St Mary's Tower. In origin, this again is early 14th century, but roughly half of it needed to be rebuilt following damage during the siege of the City in 1644.

But now back to the Abbey grounds and the remains of the Abbey itself. We mentioned before that monks from Lastingham and Whitby were given the church of St Olave. William II also granted them additional land and, in 1089, laid the foundation stone for a new and much larger church, probably of abbey proportions. Just as this building was nearing completion almost fifty years later, a fire occurred which extensively damaged both the City and the Abbey. This could be one reason why the high stone perimeter walls were started in 1266, a barrier to both fire and intrusion.

Anyway, be that as it may, rebuilding works commenced in 1270 under the direction of Abbot Simon de Warwick. It is strange to think of all those craftsmen hammering away next door to each other, one lot building the Minster and the other the Abbey. Both buildings had considerable set-backs in their history. In the case of the Abbey, lightning struck in 1377, damaging the central tower and transept. The ensuing fire also took its toll, but these were natural disasters and could be rectified. The worst was yet to come. With the latest rebuilding works completed, everything ran along smoothly until Henry VIII had his bust-up with Rome over his marital arrangements. To overcome his problems he created his own church, but this spelt doom for the monasteries, which were of course closely linked with Rome. Rather selfish of him perhaps, but then Henry was also strapped for cash, and the monasteries did own lots of land, money and treasures. So why not kill two birds with one stone?

The Water Tower

enry VII, the first of the Tudors and Henry VIII's father, had been the 'nation's housekeeper', meticulously careful with money and accounts. What could be more natural than that his son should blow the lot? In the face of the inevitable, St Mary's Abbey surrendered on the 29th November 1539. The Abbot and monks were sent packing with a pension, and the Abbot's lodging became known as the King's Manor, to be used as both palace and headquarters for the Council of the North.

As for the Abbey, it was allowed to go to seed, and later provided useful building material for subsequent purposes. We have already mentioned St Olave, but the Ouse bridge and the County Gaol also benefited.

Adjacent to the remains of the Abbey is the Yorkshire Museum which, like the Observatory, was built for the Yorkshire Philosophical Society. It was constructed between 1827 and 1829 and designed by William Wilkins with a rhythmical, striking façade. The centrepiece comprises, unusually, four Greek Doric columns supporting the portico. We liked the small but effective touch of continuing the cornice pattern around the portico. Inside, the columns revert to the more usual Corinthian type. The interior was designed by Sharp and Pritchard. The Museum contains many fragments and sculptures from the Abbey, together with early views of York. In following the path through the park we return to Museum Street. Heading north we arrive at the junction of St Leonard's Place and Duncombe Place. On the corner is the 'Red House', built in the early 18th century for Sir William Robinson, Mayor of York in 1700 and MP from 1697 to 1722; the design has been attributed to architect and woodcarver William Etty (1675-1734). Unfortunately the brickwork has been painted red, perhaps to reinforce its title. Next door, in St Leonard's Place, we have the Theatre Royal. In fact the building has existed on the site since 1744, undergoing many alterations, but what we see today is the result of a virtual rebuild in the late 19th century. At its northern end it **possesses** a very glassy appendage dating from 1968 and designed by Patrick Gwynne.

St Mary's Abbey

The De Grey Rooms adjacent were built between 1841-42, seven years after the creation of St Leonard's Place. The name comes from its creator, the Earl de Grey, and it was designed for use of the Yorkshire Hussars. It now houses the York Tourist Information Centre. It has a rather nicely proportioned stucco façade, with five imposing round-headed tall windows to the first floor. These have applied pediments to square them off, finishing with a heavily dentilled course under eaves. A light touch is given by the addition of cast-iron railings under the first-floor windows. The building was designed by G.T. Andrews.

And now, perhaps this is a convenient moment to cross the road and make our way towards the King's Manor. But which king you may ask? Why, Henry VIII of course, in whose reign the building received its name. To recap a moment, this had been the Abbot's house, founded in the 13th century and rebuilt in the late 15th century, surprisingly in brick. We say this only because brick was an expensive, scarcely used material at the time; the norm was either stone, or, in the case of other medieval dwellings in York, timber and render. Even more unusual was the use of terracotta for the window surrounds, especially as this was possibly the first use of this material for such a purpose in England. The Abbot who commissioned these works in 1483, Thomas Boothe, must have had his mind set on creating quite an individual and novel abode. We should also mention Richard Cheryholme, the builder, bricklayer and freeman of the City of York, who was contracted to do the work. His work on the house continued under William Sever, the Abbot between 1485 and 1502. It is the remains of part of this building that you see as you walk down the path towards it. The stone doorway with entablature over is c.1620, with a new-ish window to the right. No sooner had the building been taken over by the Crown than big money started being thrown at it. In fact almost £500 between 1540 and 1541 (a huge sum in those days, but considered necessary to prepare it for royal visits as well as for the Council of the North). The stone extension to the right was built between 1561 and 1570, the first of many additions that were to follow.

The King's Manor

The most extensive of these occurred at the back, and was built during the reign of James I in the 1620s. However, to backtrack slightly, by 1561 it was decided that, with the possibility of an important visit by Elizabeth I, the building needed to be brought up to scratch. Hence the expenditure of of £380 and the first extension mentioned above. From then on the floodgates opened, and no doubt Abbot Sever would have had difficulty recognizing his masterpiece after a lapse of one hundred and fifty years. Even more so as the building took a real hammering during the Civil War. It was surrendered to the 'Roundheads' on 16th July 1644. Yet more repairs!

From the King's Manor we head back past the City Art Gallery to arrive at Bootham Bar, entrée par excellence to ye ancient Citie of Eboracum, via the Roman road. If by now nature calls, there are conveniences close at hand in the base of the Bar. And now to the options. You can either start the circulatory walk around the City Walls by ascending the steps adjacent, or you can proceed with our perambulations into Area B.

But first a quick word about the gateway. How lucky we are to have it at all! In the City of London the medieval gateways were demolished in the 1760s. Bootham Bar was built near the site of a gate to the Roman fortress created to house the 9th Legion in the latter part of the 1st century. A legion comprised 5,500 men, and the fortress comprised 50 acres of land.

The present gate has its origins in the 11th century, although not much from this period remains. The bulk is 14th-century, with extensive refacing from the early part of the last century, and the turrets date from the 17th and 19th centuries. Despite this, the gate still looks convincingly ancient. The barbican disappeared when St Leonard's Place was built between 1831 and 1835. Walmgate Bar is the only gate that still retains its barbican, or outer defence. So, as with everything, there have been many changes over the centuries, both remedial and cosmetic. As we walk through the Gate, the flank walls in the passageway to left and right are all that remain from the 12th century.

And now on to Area B....

Bootham Bar

Area B

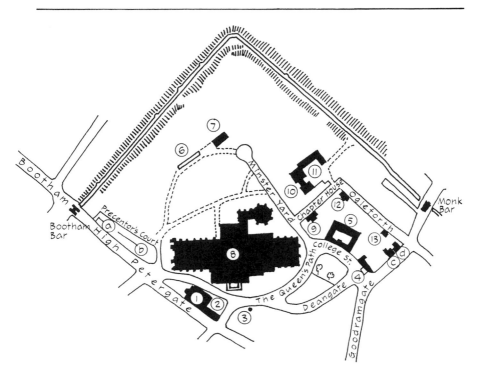

1 St Michael-le-Belfrey
2 38 High Petergate
3 Roman column
4 32 Goodramgate
5 St William's College
6 Archbishop's Cloister
7 Archbishop's Chapel
8 York Minster
9 3 Chapter House Street
10 The Treasurer's House
11 Gray's Court
12 16-20 Ogleforth
13 2 Ogleforth (Dutch House)

a The Hole in the Wall
b York Arms Hotel
c The Golden Slipper
d The Royal Oak

ootham Bar having been passed, we arrive in High Petergate, which lies on the site of the Via Principalis or main street of the Roman fortress. Petergate derives its name from the Minster. On our left, no. 8, is the only building remaining that dates from the 17th century, although some parts are older. Like a lot of the houses in York, it was re-faced in brickwork, for reasons of both fashion and durability. This may of course stem from the rebuilding of the City of London after the Great Fire of 1666, when it was realized that brick was a more practical proposition than timber and plaster. As such, and to prevent the recurrence of such a rapid spread of fire in the future, regulations were put in force to stipulate its use for all new buildings. Next door we have the Hole in the Wall public house, previously known as The Board. Beside this is a narrow passageway which leads us into Precentor's Court, a picturesque row of houses which frame the Minster perfectly. As one would expect, they are conveniently situated for the use of the precentor, whose role was that of directing the choir in the Minster. All the houses date from the early 18th century.

If we now rejoin High Petergate we come to the church of St Michael-le-Belfrey. This replaced its ancient 8th-century predecessor on the same site. This church was demolished in 1525, and the one we see today was built between 1525 and 1536, the master mason being John Forman. However, all is not what it seems, as the west front facing us was rebuilt in 1867. Fortunately this was carried out in a sensitive manner by the architect George Jones. William Etty, mentioned in Area A, put his woodcarving skills to good effect in the reredos and altar rails in 1712. The completion of the church virtually coincided with the upheaval of the Reformation, which established the Protestant religion. This then became the accepted religion in central and north-western Europe by 1563. It was in the new Protestant church that Guy Fawkes, of annually enduring fame, was baptized on 16th April 1570.

Continuing on, we come to the junction with Minster Gates and with it no. 38 High Petergate. This was built in the late 15th and early 16th centuries, originally timber-framed with a plastered jettied façade but rebuilt in brickwork in the late 18th century.

high Petergate, narrow and full of interest, invites us on. However, for a moment at least, we turn left into Minster Gates. This must be one of the shortest passages in York, but which nevertheless contains nicely proportioned brick houses with, of course, shopfronts. Should you wish, you can check the time with the clock that hangs on a bare brick wall on the right. We turn right at the end, opposite the Minster, and arrive at a freestanding column on the pavement. It was discovered in 1969 during excavations of the south transept of the Minster (the part opposite). Evidently it had stood within the Great Hall of the headquarters of the Roman sixth legion. This replaced the ninth legion in the first quarter of the second century, having accompanied Hadrian, Emperor between 117-138, on his way north. Hadrian was intent on constructing a massive boundary wall between South Shields on the east coast and Bowness-on-Solway on the west. He was a man who, with the might of Rome behind him, obviously felt that nothing was impossible (as indeed he proved, the results of his determination being visible today). To Hadrian, Britain was merely the northernmost (and probably poorest) province of the Empire; there was little to be gained, apart from security, from conquering the wet, inhospitable land that was the domain of the Picts. The line was pushed forward briefly during the reign of Antoninus Pius, but the Wall remained the definitive frontier until the departure of the Romans at the beginning of the 5th century. To return to the column, it is interesting that, rather than stone, its construction comprises very slender bricks which were subsequently rendered.

Let us now carry on along Deangate towards Goodramgate. Ahead of us lies an eye-catching landmark: a timber-framed medieval house straddling the pavement, and the only one of its type in York. The reason that it impinges on the pavement is that is was once one of the gatehouses to the grounds of the Minster.

Turning left into College Street, we see a star feature of most City guides, namely St William's College (St William being the patron saint of York). Building work started in 1465 and was completed two years later. Its purpose was to accommodate those priests whose job it was to chant masses in the Minster. In 1549 the building was granted out by the Crown. Thereafter it became the home of successive titled individuals including, in 1642, Sir Henry Jenkins.

he set up his printing presses here when Charles I moved his court from London to York during the Civil War. By the 19th century it took on both commercial and residential functions, having become divided into two dwellings with shops on the ground floor. At the beginning of this century it was sold to the Church, who then employed the architect Temple Moore to carry out restoration works. Despite alterations, it is still basically a 15th-century building and has a truly delightful courtyard which retains the flavour of that period. For more information about St William see Area F.

And now time for the open spaces. We continue northwards to the end of Minster Yard and into the grounds of the Minster. Adjoining the path is a very attractive length of freestanding arcaded stone wall showing its age. But what is its purpose? It doesn't seem to relate to anything. Well, the answer could be that it was once part of a cloister belonging to the Archbishop's Palace, of late Norman origin. Demolition of the Palace was started by Archbishop Young in the 1560s (a strange thing to do, one would have thought, but no doubt he had his reasons). Close by is a more substantial remnant, the Archbishop's Chapel. The Chapel, a simple stone box with a pitched roof, was heavily restored at the beginning of the last century, when it acquired not only the tall, narrow windows at the gable end but also its function as the Minster Library. The building was 600 years old when this happened. As with all things, someone had to fiddle about with it in the name of fashion sooner or later.

I've just realized that all this time we have been walking around with the Minster in full sight but haven't yet said a word about it. I hope that you will bear with me whilst I attempt a brief historical résumé of this most important subject.

In the white heat of the struggle to establish a new world religion, Christians gave their lives for a cause to which they were totally committed. Their unrelenting and selfless piety finally won over Romans in influential places, who perhaps saw the preaching of high moral and ethical codes as a useful adjunct to the imposition of a regulated social order, so important for a state bent on expansion and conquest.

St William's College

hat better place than Rome to spread the 'good news'? The persecutors had become the converted, and the new religion spread throughout the Empire, including the province of Britannia. But empires do not last forever, and when the Romans left in the 5th century, things started to slip back into their old ways. This state of affairs obviously needed to be rectified. So in 601 St Gregory the Great decided that the time had come to act; he would make a concerted effort to reintroduce Christianity to Britain. He therefore sent some trusted emissaries, including the monk Paulinus, from Italy to join forces with St Augustine in England. Paulinus remained in Kent until 625, when, by a happy chance for York, he was entrusted to accompany Aethelburh, sister of King Eadbald of Kent, to go there to be married to the pagan King Eadwine of Northumbria. Not long after his arrival, Paulinus was ordained Bishop of York by Archbishop Justus of Lincoln on July 21st 625. Justus had been one of St Gregory's original band from Italy.

Thus established, Paulinus began making inroads into the matter of King Eadwine's faith and, by 627, had persuaded him to drop his foolish pagan ways. The path was thus cleared for his baptism and conversion on April 10th. A small wooden church was hastily constructed for the purpose, and he and many others were baptized simultaneously. It was strange about the church, though, because the usual Christian practice was to take over pagan places of worship, rather than build their own. Humans are creatures of habit and would naturally gravitate to their usual place of worship. However, in this case, King Eadwine had become so taken with the new cause that he ordered the destruction of all heathen temples in his domains. Paulinus continued to fight the good fight with great zest and success until one fateful day in 633. On the 12th October, his staunch ally Eadwine was killed in battle near Doncaster by the combined armies of Mercia and the Welsh under Kings Penda and Caedwalla, all heathens of course. Discretion being the better part of valour, Paulinus made a hasty exit with Aethelburh and her two offspring by Eadwine. Delighted by the safe return of his widowed sister and children, King Eadbald offered the see of Rochester to Paulinus, a position he held with distinction until his death on October 10th 644. He had served his faith long and well and was obviously a man of great charisma.

So, after this brief honeymoon with Christianity, what happened back in York? Paulinus had begun to construct a new, more substantial stone church before his untimely departure, but, oddly enough and despite recent events, work on the project started again not long afterwards. The reason for this was that King Eadwine's nephew Oswald, a Christian, defeated his uncle's enemies in battle near Hexham in 634. As the new King of Northumbria, Oswald reigned until his own death in battle against his family's arch enemy, King Penda, in 642. Oswald had been a devout and highly respected man, whose remains were treasured for many centuries. Meanwhile, though, Oswald had completed Paulinus's work on the new church, a structure that lasted until the beginning of a settled line of Christian archbishops in York, starting with Ecgbert. To show how settled things had become, he and his counterpart in Canterbury, Jaenberht, even had their own coinage struck. This practice was continued by successive archbishops until 900 and 914 respectively. It was then that Edward the Elder, King of Wessex, put a stop to it. Perhaps he considered it to be an unsuitable and inappropriate activity?

However, we digress. It was in Archbishop Ecgbert's period of office, between 732 and 766, that Oswald's church was burnt down. Work started a little later on another, and much larger one during the time of Archbishop Eanbald II (796-830). This building lasted until 1069, long enough to witness the Norman invasion of three years earlier. Notwithstanding these successive calamities, work started on the next church in 1071, this time under the direction of Archbishop Thomas of Bayeux. This was to be the 'big one', a huge edifice which would form the basis of the Minster of St Peter that we see today.

Many alterations and transformations occurred between this time and its final consecration in 1472. Notable contributors in its development were Roger Pont L'Eveque, Archbishop between 1154 and 1181, and Walter de Gray between 1216 and 1255. Then of course there was the matter of the upheaval of the Reformation in the 16th century. Fortunately, in the case of York the effect of this was mainly directed at the confiscation of the Minster's treasures.

urther alterations took place in the 18th century, meant to 'tart up' the fabric, but which, in the opinion of modern conservationists, caused untold damage. Yet another fire started in the choir stalls in 1829 which spread to the vaulting. Restoration works were completed three years later. Eight years after this another fire broke out, gutting the south-west tower and burning the vault to the nave. The damaged sections were repaired by 1840.

Over a century later, great concern was caused when it was realized that the central tower was sinking and might collapse unless underpinning works were carried out immediately. Not only the tower, but the east and west fronts were also affected. The necessary remedial works started in 1968 and were completed by mid-1972 under the guidance of Bernard Feilden.

So, certainly a long catalogue of disasters. What next? In July 1984 lightning struck, and the Minster caught fire. Massive repair works were required once again. Keeping a medieval monument going certainly isn't an easy job, as architects Inigo Jones and Christopher Wren knew only too well when surveying and patching up the original St Paul's in the City of London.

What impresses is the sheer vitality and monumental scale of the Minster. The continuity of intent in the design and construction over successive centuries by each new overseer was a truly amazing feat. It was made possible by the labours of an army of wonderfully skilled craftsmen: stonemasons, scaffolding and shoring erectors, woodcarvers, painters, carpenters, tilers, leadworkers and procurers all combining to form a huge team under the guidance of the architect and, no doubt, the clergy.

Despite mass-production methods, these skills, fortunately, are still available today, and vital for maintenance and restoration works, where and when required. No doubt St Peter, for whom the Minster was named, would have been both proud and awe-struck that the religion he had helped to establish had borne such fruits. As you may appreciate, we haven't the space in this book to give an architectural appraisal of the Minster; we suggest that you purchase one of the excellent guides on your way in.

ow to return down Minster Yard, past the Treasurer's House on the left (to be mentioned in a minute), and turn left into Chapter House Street. This is a picturesque, narrow, cobbled lane with garden walls and two-storey houses. On our left, number 3 is medieval, with stone to the ground floor and render above. Originally, the upper floor was jettied, but is now cut back to the face of the ground floor. (In building terms, if the upper floors are jettied, this simply means that they project beyond the face of the floor below.)

At the end of the lane we turn left through a narrow passageway (parts of numbers 4 and 6 are of 1820s origin) and into a large cobbled courtyard. To our left is the Treasurer's House, the bulk of which is 16th and early 17th century. The windows were remodelled in 1898. Whereas the stonework elevation to the Minster Yard side presents what at first sight seems to be a symmetrical and unified design, the windows to the north and south bays are very different; only the profiles of the gabled roofscape are similar. In the courtyard the symmetry breaks down to produce a more varied and interesting series of forms. The two extreme brickwork wings do, however, echo the gables of their Minster Yard stone counterparts. A shame about all those remodelled windows though. The building was surrendered to the Crown in 1547, and was made a gift of to a private individual. A few years later it was sold on to the, by now Protestant, Archbishop Roger Holgate.

Adjoining the Treasurer's House is Gray's Court. We particularly liked the sinewy effect of the avenue of pollarded trees dividing the courtyard and leading up to the entrance. As to the building itself, the ground floor facing us was once an open gallery, flanked by six round 12th-century columns. As you see, these still exist. but the open gallery has since been enclosed by brick walls. The windows above this , as in the Treasurer's House, were remodelled in 1898, in both cases to the design of architect Temple Moore. All of the brickwork façade is c.1650, but the first-floor bay projecting over the porch is c.1900. In this the design of the windows mimics those in the wings of the Treasurer's House. The ground-floor wall to the part of the building on our right is 14th-century, but the upper floor is 18th-century. You will notice the very nicely laid out gardens to the side, that stretch out all the way to the City Wall.

A good view can be had of Gray's Court during your walk around the wall, with the gardens in the foreground and the Minster looming in the background. In fact, on this spot, one thousand seven hundred years ago, you would have found yourself looking beyond the Via Decumana towards the Principia whilst standing above the Roman fortress gateway.

But now to go back through the arch and into Ogleforth. The two-storey timber-framed houses on our right, numbers 16 to 20, were built in the 16th century. As you see, they are jettied to Ogleforth, but have acquired modern Georgian-style windows and, in keeping with our times, garage doors: a somewhat strange amalgam of old and new. The general impression in Ogleforth is that of red-brick buildings towering up on either side. These diminish, though, as we continue along the street to approach what appears to be a three-quarter-scale house on our right: a real showpiece of brickwork detailing in the Dutch style. It looks at first glance rather like an early 20th-century pastiche of an older building but, surprisingly, it is an older building, of mid-17th-century vintage and appropriately is called the Dutch House. The garage door to the side, though, does look a little more recent, and serves to emphasize the small scale of the house; one imagines that, by the time a car is parked inside, most of the ground floor would be occupied.

If by now you are ready for some liquid refreshment there is a choice of either the Golden Slipper or the Royal Oak, next door to each other round the corner in Goodramgate. Both buildings date from the 15th century, but have, of course, since then witnessed 500 years of various alterations.

But now to Monk Bar, which houses the Richard III Museum. You will find this worthy of a visit and, whilst inside, you can inspect the portcullis on the first floor and the winding mechanism on the second. The Bar is a splendid structure presenting different elevations to both sides of the City Wall. On the inside it is strictly rectangular in outline, but with the arched passageway mimicked by an arched recess on the first floor. Outside the City Wall we have a rounded appearance provided by the two turrets, both connected by a walkway at third-floor level.

Gray's Court

culpted stone figures stare down from the top of the turrets. The ground to second floors were built in the 14th century, the third being added in the 15th century. Monk Bar did have a barbican, but this was removed between 1815 and 1825; the large south-eastern arch was created in 1861. Between 1845 and 1913 Monk Bar was used as a house. We don't envy the people who chose to live there. It must have been rather cold and draughty, and did they have to use the garderobes?

Incidentally, beyond the Bar and to the north-east near Monk Bridge, a rather important facility was established in 1823. This was the York Gas Light Company. No more dark and murky streets, because, by March 1824, a supply had been laid on both to thoroughfares and shops alike. The Company also had about 250 private customers at this time. Fast work!

It wasn't long, though, before a rival company was set up, the York Union Gas Light Company. Both companies combined in 1844. From 1884, gas was also supplied to cookers and gas fires (all you had to do was hire them from the Company) a reminder of how long such domestic appliances have been with us.

But what about an electricity supply, you may ask? Well, this wasn't available for general use until 1900, when the Foss Islands Generating Works were opened.

We now set off along by the City Wall to have a quick look at the ice house, only a minute away and the start of our exploration of Area C.

Monk Bar

Area C

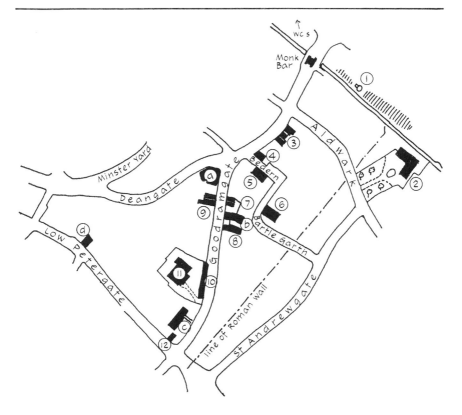

1. The Ice House
2. Merchant Taylors' Hall
3. 13-17 Goodramgate
4. 25 Goodramgate
5. Bedern Chapel
6. Bedern Hall
7. 41-45 Goodramgate
8. 49-51 Goodramgate
9. 38-40 Goodramgate
10. Lady Row
11. Holy Trinity church
12. 76 Low Petergate

a. Cross Keys Hotel
b. The Snickelways
c. Old White Swan
d. Fresheys Hotel

Coming to the Ice House, we tread a path used long ago to convey slabs of ice to its cavernous depths. But why site the Ice House in this particular spot, with no sign of lake or river nearby from which to obtain the ice in those raw winter months? Well, as it happens, the river Foss is only 300 metres or so further along the wall.

Ice houses were certainly a great idea in the days long before refrigerators. By being deep, and thus well insulated below and above ground, the ice would keep all year round: ideal for making sure that your produce remained fresh during the summer months. The Ice House dates from c.1800 and is deliberately sited on the well-drained slope. We particularly like the view of Monk Bar from this position.

Now to return to Goodramgate, where we turn left into Aldwark. Not much of interest here until we reach Merchant Taylors' Hall on our left. The Taylors' Guild was established in the late 14th century and obtained a royal charter in 1663. Looking at the building now you wouldn't guess that it was built c.1400, the reason being that the original timber-framed façades were rebuilt in brickwork in the 18th century. What with this and the modern windows, it doesn't look old or particularly interesting at all. We are, of course, referring only to the outside. The inside is a different matter, with its 16th-century tie-beam roof, later timber panelling on the walls to door height, timber and plaster upper walls and ceiling all combining to good effect.

Well, now that you've seen it, let us return to Goodramgate, where we turn left. Like many of York's great tourist attractions, this is a street which you can never tire of. Its curving nature leads one into ever-changing vistas, always human in scale and with no looming tower blocks to spoil the effect. Starting off then, on the left are three buildings of particular interest, numbers 13 to 17. Number 13 is of the late 15th. or early 16th. century, plastered and timber-framed with the first floor jettied. Number 15 is a century or so later, but again rendered and jettied. Both buildings though have ornamental Victorian gables over the windows and Victorian attic storeys. Number 17, originally 16th century but rebuilt in the 1970s, retains its rendered and jettied character.

The Ice House

Further on, at the junction with Bedern, we have number 25, in painted brickwork and of the late 17th / early 18th centuries. We may as well turn left at this point and into Bedern, a narrow passageway whose name derives from 'a house of prayer'. Rather apt because this little area once housed the Vicars Choral, whose duties lay in the Minster. Founded in 1270, the College was dissolved in 1936. On our left are the remains of a long low building, once the Bedern Chapel. Parts date from the 13th century, although, as you can see, it is in a rather sorry state. Too many bits either added or knocked away.

Moving along the lane we come to Bartle Garth, an area recently redeveloped for housing, and all very neat and tidy. The ruins of Bedern Hall, battered and derelict, could not be allowed to remain so. Fortunately, instead of being demolished, it has been renovated and now looks as pristine as the houses around it. Given a few decades, it might start to look old again. Originally built in the 14th century as the dining hall of the Vicars Choral, it formed a part of their little self-contained complex consisting of dwellings, vegetable gardens and, of course, the chapel.

Let us now retrace our steps and continue along Goodramgate, past the Cross Keys Hotel on our right and on to an ancient and attractive row of timber and plaster jettied buildings on our left. Numbers 41 to 45 look to be the archetypal late medieval house, with blackened timbers and white plaster infill. However, this wasn't how it would have looked when built in medieval times, as the practice then was to plaster over the framing. It gained its present appearance in 1929 when the plaster was removed and new windows added. This was the fashion of the day, reflected in the taste for those mock-Tudor houses that graced the stockbroker belt of many a suburb. Next door we have the Snickleways public house, of similar vintage, i.e. late 15th / early 16th-century. This time, though, the plastered frame has been retained, with windows and features picked out in red. Numbers 49 and 51. adjacent, with framing exposed in the early 1930s, are again of late medieval origin, with a splendid timber-framed hall of similar vintage at the back. On the other side of the road, numbers 38 and 40 were originally 15th-century, but were refaced and largely rebuilt in brickwork in the 17th and 18th centuries.

Lady Row, Goodramgate

Walking further along Goodramgate we arrive at York's oldest surviving houses, namely Lady Row. As one would expect, the street frontage that we now see has been altered since its beginnings in the early 14th century. However, despite new windows on the first floor and shopfronts on the ground, the row still retains its unmistakably ancient character. This is provided by the somewhat sagging jettied plaster frontage. At the end of the row is the entrance gateway to Holy Trinity church. Until the mid-17th century this site was occupied by a cottage forming the southern end of Lady Row. The view through the gate now invites you into the garden, past the weeping willow and along the snort winding path to the church, and, to complete the composition, the Minster towers are nicely framed beyond.

oly Trinity has its roots in the 12th century in what must then have been a very small building, no bigger than the present nave and chancel. We say this because so much has been added over the centuries, and not quite on the same axis as the original structure. The south-east chapel was the first addition, built in the 13th century. Then followed the south aisle a century or so later. Next came the 15th-century chapel of St James, which faces us as we approach. At more or less the same time as this, the tower and north aisle were added. The vestry at the back appeared in 1792, and in 1823 the external wall of the north aisle was rebuilt, presumably on the old foundations, otherwise the wall would have been re-set to line up with the columns of the nave. All in all, rather a hotch potch, but appealing nevertheless. The part that looks most out of character and stuck-on is one of the oldest, namely the chapel. Its slightly newish appearance is due to restoration work carried out in the early 1970s. Inside, the floor is filled with Jacobean box pews, rare survivors, which provided not only privacy but also a welcome relief from draughts. Apart from its other attractions, Holy Trinity is a known haunt for ghosts. When sitting alone in one of the pews at dusk on a wintry afternoon even the most sceptical is liable to experience cold shivers up the spine and a feeling of atavistic dread. If ever a building, by its appearance and atmosphere, deserved to be haunted, then Holy Trinity church is such a one.

Moving on down Goodramgate towards Low Petergate we see the Old White Swan on our right, approached through a small courtyard. The part of the pub fronting the street is from the 18th century, whereas the two-storey rear part, which houses the bar, is timber-framed and of the 16th century.

Next we turn right into Low Petergate, and a long sweeping vista opens up towards the Minster, interrupted only by the myriad sightseers and shoppers. Of the two jettied buildings on the right, the one at the junction with Goodramgate is early 17th-century, now with brickwork infilling the timber beams at the gable end. Next door, number 76, is two centuries earlier. Both buildings have been renovated and adapted for their present use. Most of the other buildings on this side are modern; a good moment then to cross the road to explore the other side and, with it, the start of area D.

Holy Trinity

Area D

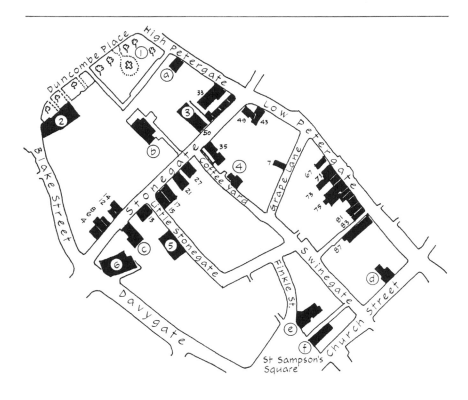

1. War Memorial
2. The Dispensary
3. Remains of Norman House
4. 2 Coffee Yard
5. Former Ebenezer Chapel
6. St Helen

a. Youngs Hotel
b. Ye Olde Starre Inn
c. The Punch Bowl Inn
d. The Golden Lion
e. The Roman Bath
f. Three Cranes

Duly crossing the road in Low Petergate from the north side, we see what's what on the south. Number 87 has its first and second floors both plastered and jettied. The side of the building faces Lund's Lane, and its constituent parts get progressively older as one passes. The street frontage, probably early 17th-century, then moves back to the 15th century and finally to the 14th-century by the time the end is reached.

Next, in Low Petergate, we see a very distinctive skyline created by a series of seven pointed gables, the buildings beneath being jettied to the street. A pity, though, about the anonymous buildings opposite, in brickwork with regularly punched holes for windows. An interesting comparison in styles.

But to take the seven gables one at a time. Number 83 is c.1600, whilst number 81 is much older, 15th century in fact. The third, number 79, almost pips Lady Row as the oldest building in York, but is late 14th-century rather than early (pretty old, though, nonetheless). The next three, numbers 73, 75, and 77, are all late 16th-century. So far we have counted six buildings, but there are seven gables. The reason is that number 75 acquired twin gables in the 17th century. As we have mentioned before about other buildings, they have moved with the times so that new shop-fronts and new windows have considerably altered their original appearance. Number 71, while not as spectacular as its plastered and jettied neighbours, is nevertheless from the early 17th century, but was refaced in brickwork in about 1800.

Poking its jettied nose out further into the street than the rest is number 67, still three storeys but not so high. It is a late 14th century structure but has been altered and renovated.

Just a bit further along on our left we come to Grape Lane, which in medieval times rejoiced in a much less innocent name. Suffice it to say that for Grape read Grope, and that the full name referred to an activity that in less explicit times gave rise to the term 'Lovers Lane'. Why this particular thoroughfare should be so honoured is not altogether clear. The oldest building in Grape Lane is number 7, late 16th-century but with a modern frontage. Old enough perhaps to have witnessed the aforementioned activity.

The Minster
(seen from behind Stonegate)

On another subject, because there are enough interesting buildings in this area to fill a book, we have in most cases concentrated on those whose origins stem from no later than the 17th century. So, our apologies to the rest!

Next, in Low Petergate, another plastered and jettied building, numbers 41-43 dating from the early 16th century. For the last jettied building in this vista we have number 33 High Petergate. The first two floors could be really ancient, the upper floors having been added in the late 16th century.

Before moving into Stonegate we should mention two other sights, both in Duncombe Place. Firstly the little open space containing the War Memorial, rather reminiscent of a medieval market cross. This is not, as you may think, a memorial to the dead of the two World Wars, but instead a remembrance to 'those loyal and gallant soldiers and sailors of this County of York who fell fighting for their country's honour in South Africa in 1899-1902'.

The other sight is a wonder of red brickwork detailing and execution of the highest order, namely the Dispensary building of 1897 by architect Edmund Kirby of Liverpool. Well worth a look. All that variety in the roofscape too. Another example of his work can be seen in Parliament Street, to be mentioned in Area F.

And so now to Stonegate, one of the prime tourist streets of York. Hardly surprising really, in view of its historic and scenic qualities. It is virtually on the same line as the Roman Via Praetoria, a road that connected the Principia, or headquarters building, at its northern end (where the Minster now stands) to the gates of the fortress at St Helen's Square. Today, though, we start with a row of mid-14th-century jettied buildings on our right. Whilst the form of the buildings is historic, the bay windows and shopfronts are relatively recent. If we take a right-hander beyond these we arrive in a small open space behind number 50. This exhibits the remains of two walls of a Norman house, quite unique in York. The structure is late 12th century, and is particularly appealing because no attempt has been made to try and recreate the past.

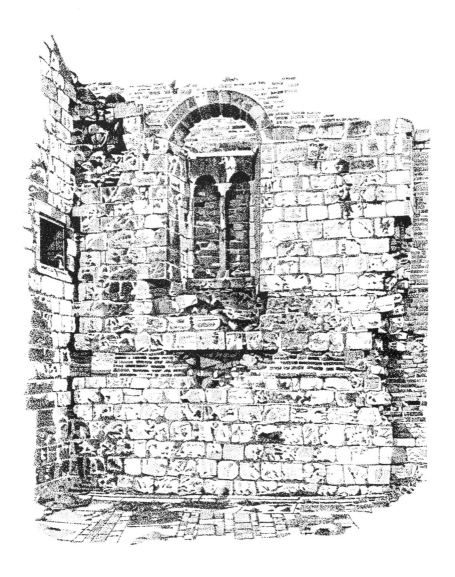

The Norman House

On the opposite side of Stonegate are two very striking buildings. Number 35 has a date of 1682, whilst number 33 boasts 1489 carved on the ornamental timber rail. According to the Royal Commission on Historical Monuments, number 35 is the older, originating from the 15th century, although all that carved woodwork, including the second-floor balcony and first-floor bay window, is late 19th century. Number 33 is c.1620 but incorporates parts of an older building. One cannot help but enjoy the flamboyance of the pair, a real asset to Stonegate.

Number 33 stands adjacent to the entrance to Coffee Yard, and sports a little red-painted gremlin perched under the first-floor overhang. In fact it represents a printer's 'devil', the name given to a printer's errand boy. No doubt he was seen darting around the neighbourhood in the early 18th century, when York's first newspaper was published in Coffee Yard. Anyway, let us explore it. On our right we pass a very attractive inset door of c.1700, and on our left Thomas Gent's Coffee House. Moving on we arrive at an open space, with number 2 on our left. It looks like a modern reconstruction of a very attractive framed and plastered medieval house, complete with timber staircase leading to a projecting first-floor entrance. The answer is that it is part reconstruction and part renovation. The early 19th-century buildings that stood in front of it have been cleared away, and the old parts revealed and restored to their former glory by the York Archaeological Trust with great effect.

The narrow passageway continues its tunnel-like route until we find ourselves back in Grape Lane. As the view always looks different on the way back let us now retrace our steps to Stonegate.

From coffee we turn now to beer, and with it Ye Olde Starre Inn, proudly proclaimed with advertising banner stretched across the street and approached through an alleyway on the opposite side of the road. So, why not make yours a pint (or two), to be added to the incalculable number served here over the last 450 years. Rather than try and describe each of the remaining buildings in Stonegate in detail, instead, we have shaded the map to show those whose origins date from the 15th to the 17th centuries.

Coffee Yard

Briefly, the even-numbered ones on the right are 17th-century, whilst those on the left date from the 15th. Naturally, as one would expect, all incorporate later modifications, but these in no way detract from the character of the street.

Before we move into Area E, a quick word about the other two remaining buildings shown on the map, namely the former Ebenezer Primitive Methodist Chapel and the church of St Helen.

The Chapel, in Little Stonegate, was designed by J.P. Pritchett and opened in 1851, but since the turn of the century has been used for more worldly commercial purposes. The design of the front is symmetrical, with arched windows at each end of the first floor. The ground floor is of rusticated stone, with white bricks to the upper two storeys, the windows having stone surrounds. But what of the Ebenezer Primitive Methodists? Presumably at the time it was built there must have been enough local members to fill its generous seating capacity. Perhaps an attempt at a summary of this particular sect would be justified.

The Ebenezer Society was founded in 1842 in Buffalo N.Y. by Christian Metz and Barbara Heinmann, immigrants from Württemberg in southern Germany. They quickly established a large following, which by 1855 numbered 800. Members were expected to sell their property as condition of joining, the proceeds going to the common fund of the commune. The Methodist ideal was founded by John and Charles Wesley in the 18th century. They were indefatigable travellers and spread their evangelical message across the country with inspired oratory. As a result Societies, formed in adherence to established rules and regulations, sprang up all over the country. Added to this, churchgoers have to thank Charles Wesley for all those popular and rousing hymns, a sure way of lifting people's hearts and uniting them in a common cause. As to the Primitive Methodists, this offshoot was founded in Staffordshire by Hugh Bourne and William Clowes. Bourne had been influenced by the revivalist 'camp meeting' approach to preaching that was so popular in America, and in 1802, he introduced a similar idea here. By 1807 he had sufficient followers to create a centre at Mow Cop on the Cheshire border near Congleton.

Stonegate

his different approach to the form of Methodist gather-
ings did not find favour with the Wesleyan Methodist
Society, of which he was a member. Obviously, strong
feelings existed in the matter, and he was expelled in 1808.
Undaunted, he, together with William Clowes, founded the
Society of Primitive Methodists in 1812.

But now to move on to the church of St Helen, at the northern
end of St Helen's Square. The font, dating from the 12th century,
is the oldest part and has witnessed the ever-changing fort-
unes of the fabric around it. These started with the rebuilding
of the church in the 14th century. The aisles were then widened
in the 15th century, and the walls of these were rebuilt again in
the 1850 s. The east and west ends date from 1857 and 1876
respectively. In 1548 the church was declared redundant, to use
a common enough phrase these days, and demolition works were
put in hand. Five years later, though, the building had a reprieve
and the parts that had been knocked down were rebuilt. By the
end of the 18th century, enthusiasm for Church of England
attendance had dwindled to an all-time low. It was only due to
to the great Victorian religious revival that many ancient and
decrepit churches were given a new lease of life. This is what
must have prompted those remedial, and sometimes over-
enthusiastic, attentions of the Victorians. The lantern, which
replaced the steeple in 1814, looks remarkably like the ones at
St Michael-le-Belfrey and All Saints, Pavement.

Well, this would seem to bring us to a convenient point to break
off and move into Area E.....

St Helen

Area E

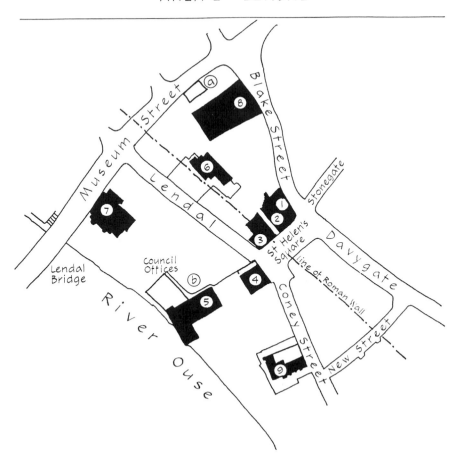

1. Savings Bank
2. Terry's building
3. Yorkshire Insurance Co.
4. The Mansion House
5. The Guildhall
6. The Judge's Lodging
7. The Yorkshire Club
8. The Assembly Rooms
9. St Martin

a. Thomas's Hotel
b. Lendal Cellars

E very night at 8·30, St Helen's Square sees the start of one of the ghost walks that are such a popular feature of the York tourist scene. They can be very interesting and informative, and visit such sites as the Treasurer's House, the King's Manor, and of course, Holy Trinity.

As to the Square itself, the Savings Bank on the corner with Blake Street turns the corner very nicely. This was designed by Pritchett and Watson, and built between 1829-30. The building is, however, given the cold shoulder on the St Helen's Square frontage by its slightly taller neighbour, the more fragmented façade of the Terry building of 1922 by Lewis Wade. Although very nicely designed in its own right, with giant Corinthian pilasters reaching up to the start of the second floor, it doesn't attempt to follow the line of the Savings Bank further into the Square. Next door we have its bulkier and more formally classical neighbour, the Yorkshire Insurance Company building of 1846-7 by G.T. Andrews. The attic dormer windows look rather lightweight and out of place compared with what happens below. They don't seem to relieve the skyline in quite the right way, if indeed it needs relieving.

On the opposite side of St Helen's Square we see a different style altogether: solid brick and stone neo-Georgian of the 1920s by T. P. Bennett and occupying the whole side. The stone pilasters above the ground floor separate red-brick panels and lead to a plain frieze with dentilled cornice above which carries on round into Davygate which is of totally modern aspect.

On the south side of the Square facing us, we see a rather colourful and stately building. It has Ionic pilasters to the two upper storeys separating bright red panels, and heavily rusticated stonework between round-headed windows on the ground floor. These are divided by a centrally placed blue painted door. The pediment boasts the Shield of Arms of the City of York. The flank wall to the right is plain rendered brickwork occasioned by the removal of its neighbour in 1884. The building we are describing is of course the Mansion House, residence of the Lord Mayors since its completion in 1730. York scored a first here with its decision to provide a specific building for this purpose, and in doing so pipped the City of London, whose equivalent was finished in 1753.

Strangely enough, the architect of York's building is not known. The chosen site for the building was occupied by the Common Hall gateway and St Christopher's Chapel, both of medieval origin, and not only involved their demolition, but also placed the Guildhall firmly out of sight. In keeping with the tradition of the piano nobile, the state room occupies the whole of the first-floor frontage, with dining and drawing-rooms on the ground floor. On the right at ground-floor level is the opening to an arched passageway, the opening rather resembling that of a missing tooth in an otherwise complete set. The passageway leads us into a courtyard and there, facing us, is the ancient front of the Guildhall, another almost symmetrical façade. The building dates from the 1450 s and replaced a smaller version.

The Guildhall was used for a variety of purposes: civic functions and meetings, the performance of plays (until 1592) and the Crown Court of Assizes. It was here that the trial of St Margaret Clitherow took place. Richard III attended a play here in 1483, the year of his accession: the subject a brief and formal summary of Christian doctrine! A hundred or so years later he could have seen Shakespeare's play about himself. We are sure that afterwards Shakespeare would not have been flavour of the month.

Unfortunately, the Guildhall suffered a direct hit in 1942, which gutted the interior. However, as you can see, this has been wonderfully restored to its original design. We now see before us a bare but very effective space, comprising two rows of five oak columns on carved stone bases, which support the roof like spreading branches. The floor consists simply of stone paving slabs, very much in keeping with the austerity of the rest, including the panelled timber ceiling. Having said previously that the Mansion House blocks the view from St Helen's Square, the Guildhall nevertheless does have pride of place when viewed from the other side of the river. All you have to do is recognize which is which when viewed alongside the adjacent Municipal Offices. We ought to add that the latter were built in 1891 and very well designed by Mawbey and Creer.

But now perhaps for a little circular tour, starting in Lendal. On our right is the Judge's Lodging which is now used as a hotel.

It was built c.1720 by and for a certain Dr Clifton Wintringham, and comprises a four-storey brick house within its own grounds (have you seen another such private house in the centre of York?). It is certainly very impressive, with, unusually, the windows to both the upper-ground and first floors based proportionally on a double square; with single square to the second floor. The door is really special: impressive stonework with carved, swagged garlands, approached by a double symmetrical stair, and this is only on the outside! No wonder it became the choice for the Judge's lodging in 1806.

Almost opposite on the other side of the road is the York Antiques Centre, well worth a browse around, and, who knows, you may even find that elusive artifact that you have always been looking for.

We now turn left into Museum Street, and on the left, we come to the Yorkshire Club, a red-brick and stone job of varied skyline with bay windows to the river frontage. The architect was C.O. Parnell, who had also designed both the Whitehall and the Army and Navy clubs in London. With this track record it is hardly surprising that he won the competition to design the Club in 1868.

Heading north towards the Minster, we pass, or perhaps call in at Thomas's Hotel for a quick one, before turning right into Blake Street. The street starts off with three large buildings. The Dispensary on the left was mentioned in Area D, and on the right we have the Registry Office of 1860 by architects Rawlins Gould. This has regular red-brick bays between stone pilasters which march smartly along the frontage. They come to an abrupt end, though, when meeting the Assembly Rooms. This building, although not so high, has plenty of character, which makes it stand out in a street that is predominantly domestic in scale. The double-height portico with Ionic columns replaced the original segmented portico in 1828. The façade is symmetrical, and the inset windows with Ionic pilasters are very attractive. The coursing of the stonework façade has been very carefully worked out using large blocks, and you will observe that the horizontal and vertical joints line through perfectly: a precision job by J.P. Pritchett and more formal than the original façade designed by Richard Boyle in 1730.

The Guildhall

The building conceived by Boyle was completed in 1735. As can be seen, alterations have occurred since then, but the Great Assembly Room is still basically as planned. It is a very impressive space, some 110 feet long and 40 feet wide, with countless Corinthian columns defining the main space, and lit from the first floor with a similar number of windows set between garlanded friezes and pilasters. One could imagine that a Roman state room might have looked something like this.

The rest of Blake Street is very domestic in character, with two-and three-storey brick houses generally from the 18th century, but interspersed with modern counterparts which tend to be three-and four-storey. Most have shops on the ground floor. Apart from the mellowed appearance, there is something about the proportion of the façades of the older buildings that distinguishes them from the others.

Carrying on to the end of Blake Street we return to St Helen's Square and the end of this mini circular tour. Next stop is the remains of St Martin in Coney Street, a street redeveloped in recent years as a main shopping artery but originally a Roman road bypassing the fortress. As we walk down Coney Street, the remains of the church are not hard to spot. You might think that the large clock, jutting out on the right in full sight, signals a jeweller's premises, but no, it is attached to the venerable remains of St Martin. The church has its roots in the 11th century, but after that hardly a century passed without new works being put in hand. This activity, designed to enlarge and enhance the church, was virtually brought to nothing when the building suffered a direct hit from enemy action in 1942. It was, however, partially rebuilt in the early 1960s, and services are still held there. A new wall was built to enclose the south aisle, a vestry added adjacent to the tower, and the remainder formed into a small garden. All in all, a very appealing asset for the street.

We mentioned Richard III earlier in connection with the Guildhall, and now perhaps we should pause for a brief word regarding this most controversial of figures, vilified by history and Shakespeare but nonetheless always held in high esteem in York.

St Martin

He was born on 2nd October 1452, the youngest son of Richard, Duke of York, and Cecily Neville, a daughter of the powerful northern landowning family. These were troubled times in England. The Lancastrian king, Henry VI, had ascended the thrones of both England and France as a minor in 1422 after the premature death of his famous father. His reign had not been a happy one. Inspired by Joan of Arc, the French had launched the long and determined counter-attack against the English possessions in France that culminated in the ruinous English defeat at Castillon in July 1453. Thereafter, only Calais remained under English rule. On attaining his majority he proved a weak and ineffectual king dominated by his formidable wife, Margaret of Anjou.

Richard of York became the focus for the opposition to Lancastrian rule and was the acknowledged leader of the Yorkist faction when hostilities broke out in 1455. After early success, his career came to an abrupt end with his defeat, capture and execution at Wakefield in December 1460 (see also Area L). His eldest son, Edward, reversed the outcome of Wakefield at the bloody Battle of Towton in March 1461, and in its aftermath Henry was deposed and Edward assumed the throne as Edward IV. Richard, now aged nine, was created Duke of Gloucester and sent north to stay at Middleham Castle, the home of his powerful cousin Richard Neville, Earl of Warwick, better known to history as the 'Kingmaker'. Middleham was the Earl's favourite residence, and it was here that Richard was groomed in those arts considered appropriate for someone who might one day be King.

Edward's throne was by no means secure, and in 1470, after plots, open rebellion, and the machinations of the Earl of Warwick, he and Richard were forced to flee the country and take refuge in Holland. In their absence, the 'Kingmaker' got Henry VI out of mothballs (the Tower to be precise) and in October 1470 reinstated him on the throne. In March 1471 the brothers returned and Richard Neville and his brother John were defeated at the Battle of Barnet on 14th April. With the subsequent defeat of Queen Margaret at Tewkesbury on 4th May and the sudden and convenient death of Henry in April, the Yorkist hold on the Crown was finally secure.

dward, king once again, appointed Richard governor of the North. Richard also gained part of the Warwick estates by marrying Anne Neville in the latter part of 1471. We say that he inherited only a part of the Warwick Estates because his older brother George, Duke of Clarence, had already married Anne's sister Isabel, her co-inheritor on the death of Warwick. Well, we all know the fate of the Duke, tried for treason by his brother Edward IV in 1477 and drowned in a butt of Malmsey wine before the sentence could be carried out.

As Governor of the North, Richard proved a very popular, respected, and able administrator. He lived at Middleham Castle and was a frequent visitor to York, at that time the capital of the north. From time to time, as Warden of the West March, he also had to call upon the men of York to support him in combating regular forays by the Scots. There were always plenty of volunteers willing to serve under his banner as he was a very able soldier and tactician.

Edward IV died in 1483, and the throne passed to his twelve-year-old son, Edward. As Edward V, his reign was rather short, so short in fact that he missed out on his coronation. In the same year both he and his younger brother Richard, Duke of York, disappeared, last being seen at the Tower of London. Richard took his opportunity. He descended upon London with a force of faithful Yorkshire followers and was crowned as Richard III on 6th July 1483.

Later that same year an ominous threat to his newly claimed supremacy appeared on the horizon in the shape of the exiled Lancastrian Henry Tudor, son of the Earl of Richmond and Lady Margaret Beaufort. Keen on grabbing the throne for himself, his first planned invasion in November 1483 never reached English shores because his front man in England, the Duke of Buckingham, was executed following an attempted co-ordinated rebellion against Richard. Henry's time came in November 1485, when he landed at Milford Haven and shortly afterwards defeated and killed Richard at Bosworth Field on 22nd November.

Richard III was the last English king to be killed in battle. His reign had lasted a little under two years.

Area F

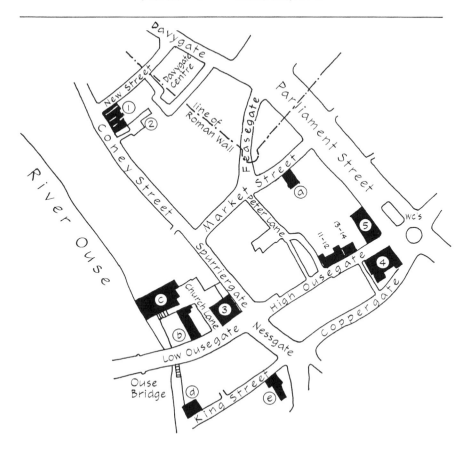

1. 16-24 Coney Street
2. Judge's Court
3. St Michael's
4. All Saints
5. Barclays Bank

a. The Hansom Cab
b. O'Neill's
c. Yates's Wine Lodge
d. King's Arms
e. The Grapes

From the bustle of new shops and buildings so far encountered in Coney Street, we are confronted by a reminder of the past with the sight of three attractive jettied buildings at the corner with New Street. The first of these, number 16, has exposed framing both to flank wall and street frontage. That to the flank wall would not have been visible originally, as a building existed alongside. This was demolished when New Street was built in 1745. Although the other two buildings retain their plastered frontages, the upper-floor windows do not look historically in keeping with the rest. But then, I suppose, neither do the shopfronts. All three buildings have pointed gables and date from the early 16th century. It is interesting to speculate how they might have looked when first built.

Just beyond these is a narrow passageway leading to Judge's Court, an early 18th-century house on three storeys with attic. The name derives from its use as Judges' lodgings from the 1750s to 1806, in which year the larger house in Lendal, described in Area E, was purchased for this use.

Market Street and Feasegate, although containing a few period buildings, nevertheless give the impression of a large modern shopping thoroughfare. This is probably because of the large shopfronts, pedestrianized brick-paved surfaces and the dominating and faceless new brick-building at the junction of the two streets. Spurriergate at Christmas sales time is filled with crowds reminiscent of spectators leaving a football match. But Spurriergate does, however, lead us on to the more interesting aspects of Low and High Ousegate. On the corner is the church of St Michael-le-Belfrey, the exterior of which dates from the 1820s, the result of street-widening to both Low Ousegate and Spurriergate. Looking at the elevations, the clock, inset at the end of the Low Ousegate façade, is an unusual feature in such a position, as it would normally have appeared on the tower. Had this been the case I think you would have had trouble telling the time. Both of the elevations are exactly the same (apart from the clock that is), a rather novel idea. Inside, though, parts of the 12th-century church still remain in the shape of the arcaded nave.

he bases to the six smaller, and original, quatrefoil columns are hidden two feet or so below ground, the floor having been raised at some stage, perhaps in the 15th century when the west bay was rebuilt. The church now houses the Spurriergate Centre.

As to Low Ousegate, all is of 1810-20 vintage, apart from Ousegate House on the corner, which is obviously later. To be counted among those victims of the street widening was a complete row of medieval timber-framed houses, on the same side as the church. On the other side of the road, the sometime owners of numbers 3 and 5 must have had a particular liking for cats, revealed by a close look at the façades.

But now to the Ouse **Bridge**, built between 1810 and 1812, the result of a competition in 1809. A recommendation had been made in 1795 that the old bridge be demolished and a new one built of iron. However, this advice was ignored, and the competition specified that the existing stone bridge, with its five arches, be repaired and widened. This brief was quickly modified when exploratory works revealed that the structure was unsound, and demolition was recommended. The competition for modifying the bridge had been won by Peter Atkinson, and his subsequent scheme for a new three-span stone bridge was adopted. His design, being rather plain and formal, has none of the glamour and interest of its cast-iron counterparts of Lendal and Skeldergate. The tradition of having had a stone bridge for so long obviously weighed heavily, but the use of cast-iron at this time would have been an exciting novelty.

The first Ouse Bridge, of timber, had collapsed under the weight of 200 or so joyous residents and clergy gathered to welcome William Fitzherbert on his return to resume his archbishopric in 1154. He had previously held this post from 1142-46, strongly supported by King Stephen (1135-54), but was forced into retirement by malicious rumours about the means by which he had gained his election. These rumours proved to be unfounded, and on this particular day, the 9th May 1154, all of that was forgotten and the people celebrated.

Apart, that is, from Archdeacon Osbert of York, who had contested William's original right to appointment in 1142 and who contested it again, this time going so far as to try to stop his entry into York. Fortunately all of those that fell into the river when the bridge collapsed survived, an occurence justifiably considered rather a miracle at the time, and no doubt the trigger for further celebrations for their safe deliverance, an outcome aided by the prayers of William. Tragically, though, William died a month later on the 8th June, supposedly from food poisoning. He was canonized in 1227 and, as mentioned in Area B, is the patron saint of York. With the collapse in mind, the next bridge was built of stone. It incorporated a chapel that was dedicated to St William in 1228. Later on, houses were built on the bridge, some of which survived until 1793.

Before leaving this corner, we would recommend a visit to the King's Arms public house, which can be seen from the bridge. This is York's famous underwater pub, so before you go make sure that flooding is not imminent! In point of fact it probably wouldn't matter, as, providing one can gain access, drinks are still served, and it all adds to the excitement. The appearance of this early 17th-century building has been transformed over the centuries, from timber-framed to brickwork, the latter having been carried out in the late 19th century. The pub is situated on the King's Staith, meaning the King's alighting place, which was the site of a quay dating from medieval times. If we were in the same place in Roman times we would be under several feet of water, as the river was considerably wider then.

We continue up King's Street to Nessgate, and then to High Ousegate. This is a brick-paved street that rises gently to the middle, then drops down to Parliament Street. Apart from a couple of narrow alleyways to be explored, it also contains two impressive 18th-century façades. On our left, numbers 11 and 12 appear as one frontage and were built during the reign of Queen Anne (1702-14). The eight windows to each floor are placed symmetrically about a central feature consisting of a pair of giant Ionic pilasters, with the first-floor window between them accentuated by a small pediment.

The King's Arms

The Ionic pilasters occur again at each end of the rendered façade. A powerful dentilled eaves caps the top off nicely. Next door, and of similar age, is a rather smaller building in the same style, although in this case the render has been removed to reveal the red brickwork behind, the result of quite successful renovation works. This time though, the pair of central pilasters are Corinthian.

And now to the church of All Saints, Pavement, on our right, most of which is of the 18th and 19th centuries. Small parts of the original 14th-century structure still survive inside, though, namely the columns and arches to nave and tower. The large lantern forms a striking landmark and was added to the tower in 1837. Inside, the stained-glass windows date from the 14th and 15th centuries. Finally a much older reminder of the church's origins, a Viking-period tomb slab, discovered during alteration works, This can be seen in the north aisle.

The last building we come to in this area (not counting the the public conveniences, if required) is Barclays Bank at the corner with Parliament Street. Painstakingly designed, detailed and executed in red, semi-engineering-quality brickwork with terracotta friezes, it is, all in all, too much to take in at a glance. We particularly like the light-hearted way in which the rainwater is taken away adjacent to the main entrance. Two gargoyles convey the rainwater into hopper heads, the gargoyles forming the springing points to a highly ornate arch over the entrance. The building was designed by Edmund Kirkby and built in 1901. There is one other similar building in York, the Dispensary in Duncombe Place, also by Edmund Kirkby and mentioned in Area D.

And now on to Area G, a part of York that every tourist has heard of and wants to visit.....

We refer of course to the Shambles.

All Saints, Pavement

Area G

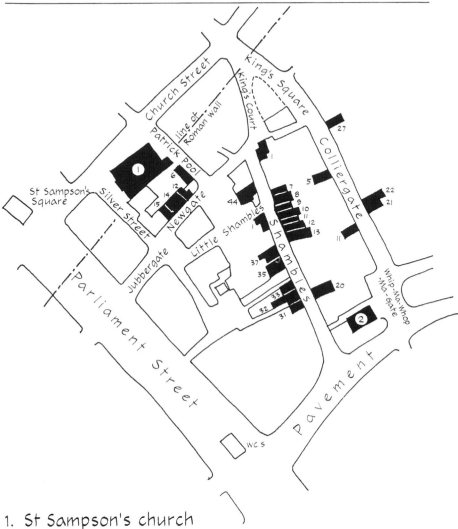

1. St Sampson's church
2. St Crux Parish Room

Going from Barclays Bank to the Shambles, our route starts with Parliament Street, a very attractive thoroughfare laid out between 1835 and 1840. The reason for its extra width is that it was designed as the new centralized market place, with the stalls occupying the middle strip: rather a nice idea. As to the appearance of the houses, strict guidelines were laid down to ensure that all were three- or four-storey, and all were to share a specific cornice design and window line. As one can see, it still retains much of this ordered treatment, and in most cases the windows do line through from one property to the next. Modern developments have not been so sympathetic, however.

At the far end we come to St Sampson's Square, mostly 18th-century buildings and including, on the south, Melrose House, a very nicely proportioned three-storey brick house of c.1770. Turning right we arrive at St Sampson's church. This was rebuilt in the early 1840s, using the existing materials to recreate the original church rather than 'Victorianize' it. Although rather small in height, it is never-theless in perfect keeping with the scale of its surroundings. But who was St Sampson? It is certainly not a name one comes across often in the naming of churches. He was of Welsh descent and born c.485, and was something of an infant prodigy in matters religious. He possessed the gift of tolerance and self-sufficiency combined with worldliness. He had a reputation as a performer of miracles, and his missionary travels took him to the Scilly Isles (one of the islands is named after him) and then to the Channel Islands and finally Brittany. He died c.565.

Turning right at the end of the church and glancing down Patrick Pool, we see an imposing and picturesque timber-framed, jettied house of late 16th-century origin. A real eye-catcher. But our route continues up Church Street, laid out in 1835, and thence to King's Square. This is a delightful little corner, domestic in scale and with great variety on all sides. No two buildings are the same, and all would have witnessed the demolition of Holy Trinity church in 1937. This had previously occupied the central, and now leafy, part of the Square. In Roman times we would have been standing at a very busy spot, as we are on the site of the south-eastern gateway to the legionary fortress. The Square is also a meeting place for the various ghost walks on their nocturnal perambulations.

Patrick Pool

f we now bear right to the south-west corner we come to the Shambles, parts of which conjure up the image of what a lot of York's streets must have looked like three hundred years ago. Jettied buildings almost touch each other across the street, and one wonders how much privacy there can have been when it was possible to look directly into your neighbour's bedroom window opposite; and did people really expect to get covered in you-know-what as they walked past? It's one thing to receive a direct hit from one of our feathered friends, but quite another to get plastered with the other.

The Shambles, so named because it was the traditional centre of the butchery trade, is a place to be experienced, so rather than describe each building in detail we have instead shaded the map to show those that are of 14th- and 15th-century origin. Number 13 is an exception being early 17th-century, whilst number 20 dates from the 18th.

One house we must mention is number 35, now a shrine to Saint Margaret Clitherow. According to the Royal Commission on Historical Monuments, she actually lived at number 10, almost opposite. Margaret was born in 1556, daughter of Thomas Middleton, a freeman and sheriff of York between 1564-5. She married John Clitherow, a glazier and butcher, in 1571; both were Protestants. Two or three years after her marriage, however, she adopted the Catholic faith, a highly dangerous thing to do in the reign of Queen Elizabeth. Her very tolerant husband chose to turn a blind eye to this, even though he was fined for his wife's continued absence from church. This absence, combined with the suspicion that she was harbouring Catholics, resulted in a two-year prison sentence for Margaret. Having served her term, and still unrepentant, she continued to follow her faith and used part of her home for Mass, as well as giving shelter to priests. This was a heinous crime at a time when the state was determined that the entire population should embrace the recently established Protestant Church of England. People were even tried and executed because they refused to make the change. Margaret became one of these victims and was arrested again in 1586 and taken for trial at the Guildhall. She refused to plead, a crime automatically punished by being pressed to death.

The Shambles

She maintained that she had no crime to answer for, and that being guilty or not guilty was, in terms of Christian belief, a ridiculous charge. So the sentence was carried out, by one Christian on another. She was beatified in 1929 and canonized in 1970, not before time one might think.

Now on into the Little Shambles where you will find an open market to browse around. If you glance back to the Shambles you will see a view equally as quaint as any that we have seen. The butchers haven't vanished altogether; they have moved into the market instead.

Returning to the Shambles and walking to the end, we arrive at Pavement. To our right is Marks and Spencer, and to our left the St Crux Parish Room, a modest single-storey stone building with a slate roof. The building is relatively new, being built on the site of the church of St Crux, demolished in 1887. Materials from the old church were used in the construction of the building we see now. It does look a little apologetic in comparison with its magnificent early 15th century predecessor, and one wonders why the trouble was taken to demolish the church only to build something much smaller in its place.

Behind St Crux is Whip-ma-whop-ma-Gate, a long, wonderfully eccentric name for such a short thoroughfare. This leads towards Colliergate, a street of attractive brick houses mainly of three storeys. The first five-bay house on our left is c.1725, whilst the one opposite with the heavily dentilled eaves is about forty years later. Most of the buildings are 18th-century, and those that had been timber-framed were refronted in this period. The single exception is number 5, which retains its jettied elevation. We have shaded the map to show those buildings that were 16th- and early 17th-century timber-framed but subsequently refronted in brickwork. By the time we reach King's Square, the buildings on the right date from the 19th century. It is a great pity about the double yellow lines running the length of Colliergate, they always look very intrusive in old streets with a lot of character.

Anyway, having now reached St Andrewgate, the time has come to move on into Area H......

Little Shambles

Area H

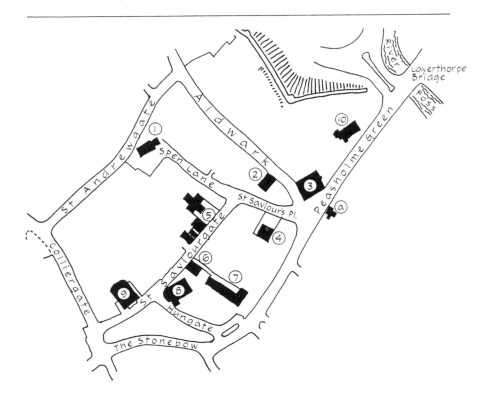

1. St Andrew's Hall
2. Former Wesleyan Chapel
3. St Anthony's Hall
4. Peasholme House
5. St Saviourgate Chapel
6. Lady Hewley's Hospital
7. Lady Hewley's Almshouses
8. St Saviour
9. Centenary Methodist Chapel
10. St Cuthbert

a. The Black Swan

aving a glance at the map for this area, it would seem that it does not contain as much of interest as the others. Well, all we can do is set off and see. So, carrying on from Area G, we proceed up St Andrewgate, with not much of interest until we reach St Andrew's Hall. What can one say? It is a building that was probably interesting once, when it was used as a place of worship before being made redundant as long ago as the 16th century. Since then it has served a multitude of uses, as a stable, a brothel, a school, a cottage and, lastly, a meeting house for the Christian Brethren Despite restoration, wouldn't you feel a bit jaded after all that?

Opposite, as we see, the area around Bedern has been rebuilt extensively for new housing, a welcome alternative to the endless office developments of most city centres.

But now to turn right into Aldwark, a continuation of the part we visited in Area C. A long walk alongside much new housing brings us eventually to numbers 40-42 on our right. This is now a warehouse, but it was originally built as a Wesleyan chapel in 1759. Strangely enough, it was only used as such for forty six years. Still, it does have a particular distinction, in that it was opened by John Wesley, and he preached the first sermon.

On arriving at the end of Aldwark we come to a junction, with Peasholme Green and St Anthony's Hall on our left. This building is an attractive combination of brick and stone. The stone part, on the ground floor, is mostly 15th century on the Aldwark side, and 17th century on the Peasholme Green elevation. The brickwork upper storey is all of the 17th century. The building started life as a chapel for the guild of St Martin and was consecrated in 1453. It was also used as a hall by other guilds who lacked their own. The original guild lasted until 1627. From then on it served a variety of functions and was obviously popular, for, by the 1650 s, the upper storey had been added. The longest occupants were the Bluecoat school, from 1705 to 1946.

Turning sharp right we are in St Saviour's Place, with, on our left, an imposing residence of four storeys, namely Peasholme House which dates from 1752.

uilt in brickwork, it has a very pronounced dentilled eaves, and the proportions don't seem to be conventionally Georgian. The second-floor stone banding sits uncomfortably close to the cills of the second-floor windows creating a large gap which separates them from what happens below. The lintels are in gauged brickwork but, unusually, have rather pronounced stone keystones which give the building a novel and idiosyncratic appearance. The brickwork facade isn't allowed to flow naturally around the sides. Instead it is stopped by the stone quoins that frame the elevation. The building is approached via an open courtyard, a space occupied until twenty years or so ago by a warehouse that obscured the building from the street. The York Civic Trust were responsible for the restoration of the building, attributed to one of York's foremost Georgian architects, John Carr.

Continuing up the street we turn left into St Saviourgate Anyone looking for a residential street encompassing the span of the Georgian era from the 1720s to 1780s would be hard put to find a more representative selection.

The gap on our right proclaims the courtyard of the Unitarian Chapel, built in the form of a Greek cross in 1692. The building is unique in York in that it was the first Nonconformist place of worship in the City. It was originally Presbyterian. This was of course twenty years or so before the Wesley brothers began their crusade in Oxford for what they believed would be a more popular approach to the methods of preaching Christianity. The chapel is the oldest building in this part of St Saviourgate.

Carrying on, we arrive at the church of St Saviour. This was made redundant as a place of worship in 1954, and now houses the ARC, also known as the Archaelogical Research Centre. The church was built in the 1450s, although all that now remains from that period is the tower and the internal columns with arches defining the nave and chancel. The north and south aisles were rebuilt in the 1840s, with the vestry added thirty years later. The stone tower, with symmetrical gables either side, forms a satisfying composition.

Adjacent to the church, in St Saviourgate, we see a small two-storey stone building. This is Lady Hewley's Hospital, which was designed by J.P. Pritchett and built in 1840. It replaced the original hospital building that was founded in 1700. Lady Sarah Hewley (1627-1710), was the heiress to a fortune that had been amassed by her father, Robert Wolrych. Her mother had also inherited a fortune from her first husband, and consequently Sarah became a very wealthy woman. She married John Hewley, Recorder of Doncaster, who was knighted in 1663. Both husband and wife were Presbyterian, and it was he that built what is now the Unitarian church described earlier. After his death in 1697, Lady Hewley contributed large sums of money to charity, including the establishment of the hospital and almshouses. These were rebuilt at the same time as the hospital, and the row of them can be seen nearby.

Slightly further along on the right we come to a very large and imposing edifice, with a portico comprising four giant Ionic-order columns with a plain pediment over. The main elevation is of brickwork with stone pilasters, the windows also having stone surrounds. All in all, it is a simple design but, because of its scale, it looks very powerful. It was designed by James Simpson and built in 1840. The date is significant, as it is the Centenary Methodist Chapel.

Opposite is a large 1960s development, Stonebow House, which is contoured to follow both the triangular site and the slope of the road. It incorporates some rather uninviting spaces. This rather bullish building is clad in pre-cast concrete panels with exposed stone aggregate, with the concrete beams and columns designed to mimic timber post-and-beam construction. It was designed by architects Hartry, Grover and Halter and received considerable acclaim when first built, but is not highly regarded now, probably because it does not pay much respect to its surroundings.

The Stonebow is a thoroughfare created since the last war, and leads us back to Peasholme Green.

St Saviour

Opposite St Anthony's Hall, described earlier, we have the Black Swan public house. A brief historical description by the door lists some notable York dignitaries who have lived here since the early 15th century. The twin gables are the oldest part, originally dating from the late 16th century, but now have the plaster removed to reveal the timber framing. The dormer to the right looks as though it should have a window in it, otherwise why have it?

Continuing along Peasholme Green, we come to the church of St Cuthbert on our left. It was mentioned in the Domesday Book, and indeed a small part of the church from this early date still exists in the east wall. The extent and outline of this older stonework is still clear to see, as the coursing is much smaller than that adjacent. The rest is mainly early 15th century, when it was rebuilt by William Bowes (who, as you will have noted, was one of the earlier residents of the Black Swan). The inside of the church is unusual in that it consists of one uninterrupted space, rather than being subdivided in the normal way by nave and aisles. This feature has in recent years been taken advantage of by the installation of a 'building within a building'. Visitors will see what we mean. The vestry is a Victorian addition.

A bit further on, to our left, we see the end of the City Wall. There is a four hundred metre gap in the circuit of the wall extending from Peasholme Green to the Red Tower. The reason for this is that in medieval times this was very marshy ground with the River Foss meandering through it.

And so, on reaching the Layerthorpe Bridge, we arrive at the start of Area I.

The Black Swan

Area 7

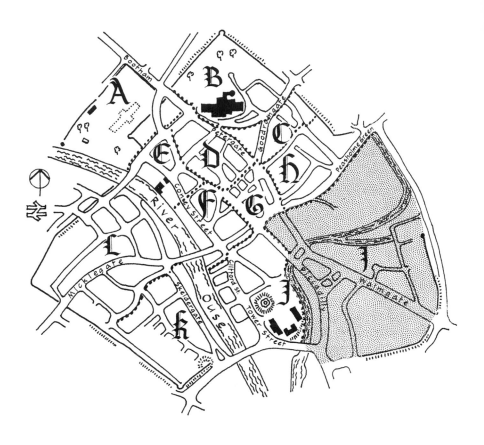

1. Rowntree Wharf
2. 20-22 Fossgate
3. Lady Peckett's Yard
4. Merchant Adventurers' Hall
5. St Denys
6. St Margaret
7. Bowes Morrell House
8. Walmgate
9. The Red Tower
10. Fishergate Bar
11. St George's churchyard
12. St George's church
13. Fishergate Tower

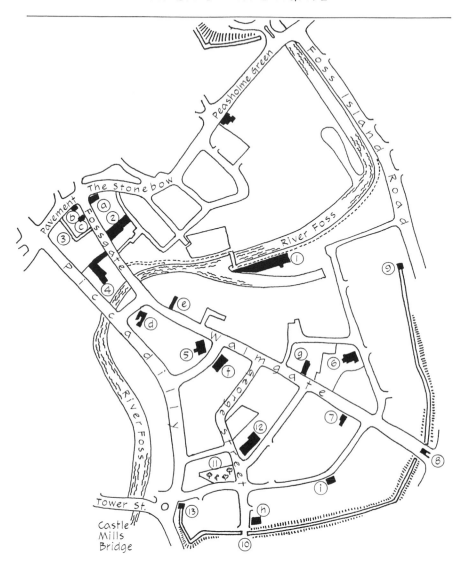

a. The Northern Wall
b. The Golden Fleece
c. The Blue Bell
d. The Red Lion
e. The Five Lions Hotel

f. St Denys Hotel
g. The Spread Eagle
h. Phoenix Inn
i. The Brown Cow

In this section we are on the outskirts of the walled city area, the industrial belt in fact-all part of York's varied pageant. Let us carry on southwards with a walk alongside the brown, murky depths of the River Foss. At the bend in the river we leave the road and take to the towpath. Two hundred metres or so later we arrive at a large and attractive late 19th century warehouse building, now converted for residential use. This is Rowntree Wharf, the name Rowntree being very familiar in the realms of chocolate and confectionary manufacture. The company was founded in 1862 by Henry Isaac Rowntree. One of the family, Benjamin Rowntree (1871 - 1954) is well known as both sociologist and philanthropist. He put his views on social welfare to good use in the family business by introducing both the concept of the five-day week and an employee pension scheme. He also carried out extensive surveys on working-class conditions in York, and published his findings on three occasions: in the late 1890 s, in the 1930 s, and finally in 1951.

Fortunately, a footbridge has been built over the river in recent years, and so we are now able to take a short cut over it and thence back towards the centre of town. We pass by the side of a new three-storey car park in light brown brickwork with red banding on our right, and are then confronted by a very pleasant view of the Foss Bridge a bit further along. After turning right, a short walk through some narrow alleyways brings us to Fossgate. The street is paved with granite setts, and nearly all of the buildings are of brick and generally three storeys. Here you will find plenty of shops, including many new and secondhand bookshops. A little way along, on our left is a brick building with a Dutch gable and a coat of arms over the doorway. This is a largely rebuilt copy of the original 17th-century gatehouse to Merchant Adventurers' Hall, the entrance being wedged between an antiques shop on the left and model shop on the right. The Hall, which will be described later, lies immediately behind.

Slightly further up the street, on our right, is a fantastic façade, which by no stretch of the imagination, pays any regard to the traditional style of its neighbours.

Foss Bridge

Although now owned by Macdonalds (furniture, not beefburgers), it was built in 1911 and formed the entrance to the Electric Theatre, designed by W.H.Whincup. The vast central niche is supported by four Ionic-style columns, the whole clad in faience tiles and sporting a snarling face as the centrepiece. Its exuberant design perfectly reflects the novelty of the new medium of entertainment. A contrast of old and new can be seen with the timber-framed and jettied façade of numbers 15/16 a couple of doors along. This a late 16th century house, which, with number 8 further along, is a last survivor of many such that must have once lined Fossgate. It remains, nevertheless, a narrow and very appealing street, largely because of the variety of both buildings and shops.

On arriving at Pavement we have the Northern Wall public house (built to replace the Board Inn of late 16th. century origin but demolished in 1957) on one side and the Army and Navy Stores on the other. This side of the short stretch of Pavement contains much of interest. Starting with the most obvious, we see a large, twin-gabled, jettied, timber-framed building sagging towards the centre and forming an eye-catching landmark. This is Herbert House, built in the early 17th century, but which would have looked completely different before 1926, when the original plaster covering the frontage was removed to expose the the timber framing. This seems to have been a popular pastime in that era, and was evidently done to demonstrate what people thought a real timber-framed building should look like. Certainly it was a popular style, and mock-Tudor buildings graced many a suburb in the 1920s and 30s. One has to admit that they wouldn't have looked quite so distinctive if plastered over. One imagines that the original buildings were plastered to give added insulation during our cold English winters . The cottages in Lady Row give an idea of what most medieval buildings would have looked like. The Golden Fleece public house, next to Herbert House, was once an integral part of it and incorporated the third gable. However, it has been refronted in brickwork, and the gable is no more.

Merchant Adventurers' Hall
The gatehouse in Fossgate

One of the most attractive alleyways in York can be found by turning sharp left through the archway at the far end of Herbert House. Passing under the building we enter Lady Peckett's Yard, a narrow passageway with steps, its period atmosphere highlighted by the splendid jettied 16th-century row on our left. The vista is nicely closed by a 17th-century brick building, built over a short lane which bears left to link up with Fossgate.

But now to step back to Pavement, where we turn left and then left again into Piccadilly. At first glance, everything seems very new and mostly retail and commercial. Not far along however, on the left, we arrive at a sunken garden containing the Merchant Adventurers' Hall, a long double-gabled building that was constructed between 1357 and 1361. The undercroft is of brick with stone surrounds to the windows, and the Great Hall lies behind the timber-framed upper floor. Once again, the plaster covering to the timber framing was removed in the 1920s. The stone chapel at the far end was added in the 15th century. Inside, the Hall is a magnificent space, the intricate web of timbers supporting the double roof bearing down upon what seem to be remarkably slender central timber columns. The building was constructed for the Guild of our Lord Jesus Christ and the Blessed Virgin Mary. By 1430, though, this guild had become the Merchant Adventurers, who traded extensively in the export of cloth to the Netherlands. The English wool industry was for several centuries the economic staple of the country, and the guild flourished, having a virtual monopoly of the trade up until the 17th century.

Carrying on, we perhaps pause for a few moments to admire the view towards the Foss Bridge, and then pause again at the Red Lion public house around the corner in Merchantgate. You will note, from the description on the wall, that this is the oldest building in York to hold a licence, and that, with various extensions, it dates from the 15th to 17th centuries. It is certainly a very attractive timber-framed hostelry, particularly if you enjoy a pint of John Smith's ale.

Lady Peckett's Yard

And now to Walmgate, a varied streetscape somehow typical of many seen in other towns. We wonder what the Romans would have thought of it. What had happened to their perfectly straight Via Principalis, starting at the fortress gate by King's Square and passing through Walmgate? For them Fossgate and Walmgate would have definitely seemed to have strayed off course.

Our first stop, though, is St Denys on the right. Churches have existed on this site since before the Norman Conquest, but that which we see today is an amalgam of additions and alterations that commenced soon after the rebuilding of the church in the 14th century. This activity finished with the tower, which was rebuilt in the middle of the last century. The reset doorway, though, is 12th-century, but more about this in a moment. Oddly enough, the next church we visit, that of St Margaret, also seems to have received the same treatment. When viewed from Walmgate it is seen sitting in a grassy churchyard with a few old tombstones dotted around. The church is unusual, though, in that the tower is mainly of brickwork, with stone quoins and castellated parapet, whereas the body of the church is of stone. The tower is the oldest complete part, and was built in the late 17th century. The rest, although first mentioned in the 1180s, is a mixture of periods starting in the 14th century and ending in the last century. Despite this, it retains a simple unity of appearance, and, like St Denys, it also has a reset Norman-period south porch, but this time a fine elaborately carved example. Both were transferred to the two churches from the remains of St Nicholas without Walmgate, the last vestiges of which had gone by 1736.

Further along on the other side of Walmgate we find a building that looks somewhat out of place, being adjacent to a modern three-storey brick terrace with shops and a new housing estate behind. Despite the exposed timber-framing on the front, is it really old or simply a pastiche? Are the one-pane metal windows in character? This is the Bowes Morrell House, described on a tablet on the wall by the door as one of the best examples of a late 14th-century timber-framed house.

Walmgate Bar

We suppose it might have been, once upon a time, but that time was probably some time ago-certainly well before 'restoration' works began. In fact the 17th-century rear section in brickwork looks more authentic. The building is named after John Bowes Morrell, founder chairman of the York Civic Trust, who was presumably involved with the first renovation works of 1932, but not the second of 1966, the results of which we are sure would not have met with his approval.

Now on to Walmgate Bar, our next port of call. Instead of an obviously defensive-looking building, we are confronted by a structure that looks decidedly domestic in character. As can be seen by a glance at the surrounding masonry, this appears to be a fairly recent appendage. Surprisingly, it is rather old (late 16th-century in fact) and survived heavy bombardment during the Civil War in 1644. Admittedly the cannon fire was directed from beyond the city at the outer defences. We can see these by walking through the gate, and what a treat to find the barbican, or outer defence, still intact. Walmgate Bar was built in the 14th century, and as you can see has been well maintained ever since. The Civil War damage was rectified almost immediately. Not surprising, considering that in those days you never knew when you might be attacked again. Should you wish, a diversion can be made by turning left and walking along the wall to visit the Red Tower. This is a square, brick box with walls a metre thick and built c. 1500. At that time it was taller and probably had a castellated parapet, and would have been surrounded by the marshy waters of the river Foss.

To pick up on our route again, we turn right at Walmgate Bar and continue along the wall to the Fishergate Bar. This is a much more modest job, in fact not much more now than an opening in the wall. It wasn't always thus however. When first built, in the early 15th century, it had both a tower and a portcullis. The stone steps we now use to descend to the road on one side and then up the corresponding set on the other, were added in 1827. The arched opening, which had been blocked in since 1490, was reopened in 1827 too.

Fishergate Tower

A short walk up George Street brings us to what is now a public garden, but, as you see from the tombstones dotted around, was once a churchyard, that of St George. This is not to be confused with the Roman Catholic church of St George nearby, built in 1850 and designed by Joseph and Charles Hansom. Our churchyard once contained a medieval church, the last remnants of which disappeared in the 18th century. Some things that presumably have not disappeared are the remains of John Palmer, alias Dick Turpin, the notorious highwayman. Richard Turpin was the son of John Turpin, landlord of the Bell public house in Hampstead. Dick was sent to be apprenticed to a butcher in Whitechapel, and, having served his term of apprenticeship, then returned to already familiar territory at Epping in Essex. Soon after starting his trade he married a certain Miss Palmer. His business proved very lucrative, the meat being purloined from the livestock of local farmers. In order to enhance this still further, he joined forces with a gang of deer poachers. Deer stealing with the 'Essex gang' led to stealing from people's houses, usually at gunpoint. Their notoriety and success at this new venture became such that a reward of £100 was offered for the capture of any one of the gang. In the circumstances they split up, and Turpin moved to new pastures in Cambridge. It was there that he met and joined up with the highwayman Tom King. After a series of robberies both in Cambridge and Lincoln they then sought new avenues in London. News spreads fast however, and they were ambushed at the Red Lion in Whitechapel. In the ensuing fracas King was accidentally shot and killed by Turpin. After this he assumed the name of Palmer, mounted his trusty steed Black Bess and, as legend has it, galloped off on his epic ride to York. Being unknown there, and with the large amount of money that he had gained from his previous exploits, he was able to live the life of a country gentleman for a while. That is until he made threats against his landlord. He was arrested, and his background checked. Whilst imprisoned in York Castle, witnesses were summoned from Cambridge and Lincoln who identified 'Palmer' as Dick Turpin. He was tried on the 22nd March 1739 and executed on the 7th April.

Dick Turpin's Grave

aving seen the churchyard, we now move on down Lead Mill Lane to arrive at the Fishergate Tower. The tower, which was built between 1504 and 1507, is a rectangular, stone structure of great character, and forms a fitting end stop to this section of the City Wall. There is something about the shape of it, with its small, strictly spaced windows under the eaves, its stone bulk punctuated by a minimum of openings, that gives it a rather unusual appearance. Also, the tiled roof could not be more appropriately shaped to form the perfect cap to the structure below. The adjacent tree is perfectly positioned to create a very pleasant composition.

And, with this, we head off across Castle Mills Bridge and into Area J.

Area 3

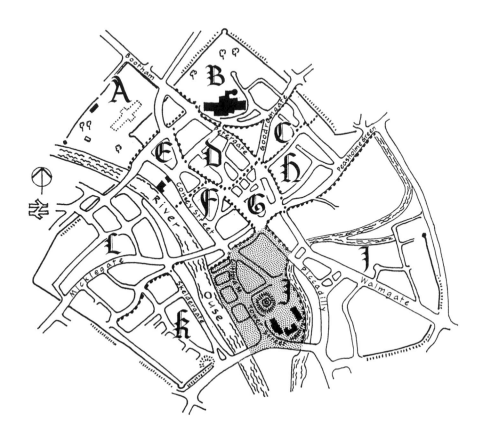

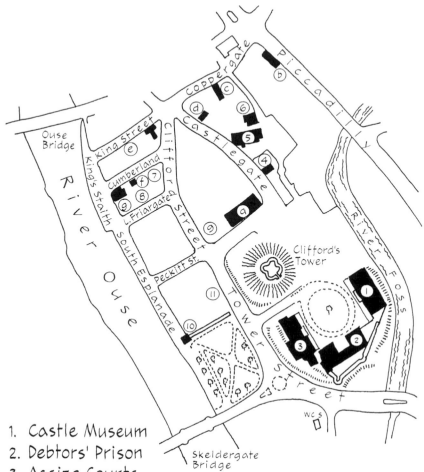

1. Castle Museum
2. Debtors' Prison
3. Assize Courts
4. Fairfax House
5. St Mary (The York Story)
6. Jorvik Viking Centre
7. York Dungeon
8. Friargate Wax Museum
9. Regimental Museum
10. Davy Tower
11. Museum of Automata

a. Stakis York Hotel
b. White Swan Hotel
c. The Three Tuns
d. The Little John Inn
e. The Grapes Inn
f. Plonkers
g. Lowther Hotel

Just a few hundred years ago we would have found ourselves crossing a dam, surrounded by water, to get to York Castle from Fishergate Tower. As we approach, the first building we see on our right doesn't look like a castle at all; in fact it is the side of the former female prison, now the Castle Museum. Further along, though, we do see the Castle-or rather the bailey wall, which looks more the part. Up until the middle of the 18th century the Castle still retained all of its original enclosing walls, but, a hundred years later, most had been demolished leaving only a small section to the south that we pass on our way to the Museum.

On arrival we find ourselves confronted by a large oval expanse of grass with a rather solitary tree in the middle. To our left is the Museum building which was built between 1780-83 and designed by Wilkinson and Prince. The façade, in sandstone, is virtually a mirror image of the building opposite and to our right, namely the Assize Courts. This dates from 1773-77, and was designed by John Carr. The rear section was extended in the early 19th century by Atkinson and Philips. Both buildings have symmetrical façades around a triangular pediment supported by four Ionic columns, all of which form a screen to the inset porch. The Ionic theme is taken up again with four pilasters marking the ends of the façades. There is a difference between the two buildings, though; the Assize Courts boast giant-scale statuary at parapet level, which comprise a figure of Justice, a lion, a unicorn and two urns.

Facing us across the square is the Debtors' Prison, built between 1701-05 (architect unknown) and designed originally as the County Gaol in the English Baroque style. Again this is a symmetrical design, and, because of its rather stately appearance, does not look quite as one imagines a prison should. This could not be said of a large-capacity institutionalized prison that was built in 1835 which comprised a round central administration building from which the accommodation wings radiated, the whole separated from the square by high walls.

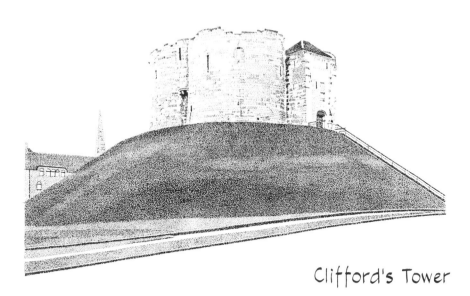

Clifford's Tower

The Castle Museum is well worth a visit. It contains a wealth of everyday artefacts from many periods, and rooms have been decorated and furnished, complete with dressed models, to show the changing tastes in fashion over the decades. There are also reconstructed period shops, with goods displayed, and workshops displaying the skills of the craftsmen before the age of mass production. All in all, a very broad and fascinating collection. And, of course, you can also visit the condemned cell, once a place of terror and anguish but now an object of idle curiosity.

We now leave the great indoors and return to the great out-doors to visit Clifford's Tower on the other side of the square. The grassy mound on which it sits was created between 1068-9 during the reign of William the Conqueror. It originally had a timber fortification on top, and the mound was separated from the Castle by water up until the early 18th century. Before 1935, the only way we could have visited the Tower would have been if we paid admission or were serving a stretch 'inside', as a ten-metre-high wall enclosed both it and the 1835 prison mentioned earlier.

owadays we are free to climb the steps to the Tower, having first read the chilling plaque recounting the fate of some 150 Jews of York, who, having sought protection in the castle previously on this site, committed suicide on the night of the 16th March 1190, rather than suffer at the hands of a mob incited by Richard Malebisse. The quatrefoil stone structure we approach was built between 1245-62 by order of Henry III (1216-1272 : a long reign surpassed by only George III and Queen Victoria). The Tower was assigned the role of 'Fort Knox' in the 14th century, but this function was short-lived, because two centuries later both the Tower and Castle were in ruins. Demolition work, or more properly the removal of stonework, was started by Robert Redhead in 1596, but his activities were halted following action by the city council. Fifty years or so later it was tarted up and served as a barracks to house Royalist forces in the Civil War. When York surrendered in 1644 it continued to be used for this purpose during the period of the Commonwealth and subsequently during the reign of Charles II. All came to an end, though, in 1684, when it caught fire. From then on it served only ornamental purposes until being encompassed within the prison complex described earlier. Now it is a worthy tourist attraction with panoramic views of York from its parapet. It is from here that we see our next objective, Fairfax House in Castlegate, to the right of the new Stakis Hotel building.

This is a three-storey house of strictly Classical proportions in red brick, with stone surrounds to the windows, stone banding and a large pediment. It was designed by John Carr and completed in 1763 as the residence of Charles, Viscount Fairfax of Elmley. The interiors are most noteworthy, including some wonderfully decorative ceilings displaying all the skills of the plasterer's art. The consistency of quality is carried through to the equally elaborate wrought-ironwork to the staircase balustrading. The triumphal pilastered arch on the half-landing provides a strong feature in what is an otherwise simple space. Also of note is the fine carving to the doorways to be seen as you walk round the collection of Georgian furniture displayed in appropriate domestic surroundings.

From Fairfax House we now cut around the block and into a new shopping precinct named Coppergate Walk. On our left in the square we have St Mary's church, now playing host to 'The York Story'. Have you ever seen such an outlandishly high and finely tapered tower? Quite an amazing creation. The church predates the Conquest, although hardly anything from this period now remains. A dedication stone was discovered in 1870, which dates from the 10th or 11th centuries. The bulk of the church, though, is of the 15th century.

Next door to St Mary's is a new building with, usually, a long queue of people waiting to enter. You had better be quick, then, to take up your position to visit the Jorvik Viking Centre. During excavations under Coppergate remains of the Viking occupation of York during the 9th and 10th centuries were discovered. The remains included everyday artifacts as well as parts of original structures. Interiors and tableaux from the life of the times have been created to give a feel of what York might have been like during that time. One wonders whether two thousand years hence there might be a similar exhibition on our times.

But back to the Vikings, the collective name for the Danish and Norwegian raiders who spread terror through Northern Europe for over two centuries. Their first recorded raid on England was at Lindisfarne in 793, and in the following years they increased in range and frequency. At first these raids were purely for plunder, but in time they became the prelude to a more permanent conquest. At this time the Anglo-Saxons, who had themselves changed from ferocious raiders of Roman Britain to permanent settlers, were divided into separate kingdoms. These were Northumbria, Mercia (in the Midlands), East Anglia, and Wessex in the south. The first major Danish invasion came in 865 when they landed in great force on the shores of East Anglia. They then moved north-west via Nottingham and Lincoln, and occupied York. An effort by Osbert, King of Northumbria, to half the advance was unsuccessful, and by the year 867, the Danish invaders had swallowed up the rest of his kingdom as well.

espite repeated efforts the Danes never succeeded in conquering Wessex, and were beaten once and for all by Alfred the Great at Edington in Wiltshire in 879. This victory signalled the beginning of a fight-back by the Anglo-Saxons to reclaim their lost territory. It was King Aethelstan who brought English rule back to York in 927, and his conquests throughout the country resulted in his being recognized as King of all England. He ruled between 924 and 939. His successors, Eadmund and then Eadred were harassed by further threats to York, this time from Eric Bloodaxe (the name speaks for itself). Eadred finally solved the problem by expelling Eric in 954.

Another Danish invasion came in 1013, when Swein Forkbeard, after conquering the north, marched south sweeping all before him. Even Wessex fell. He died in 1014 and his son Cnut (Canute) took over. After initial defeat and flight to Denmark, he returned and defeated Edmund Ironside in 1016, becoming King of all England and reigning until 1035. Danish rule ended with the death of his son Harthacnut in 1042, when the throne passed to the Saxon, Edward the Confessor. His successor, Harold II Godwinsson, was faced with yet another invasion in 1066, this time by his brother Tostig and the Norwegian king, Harold Hardrada. The northern earls were defeated at Fulford and York captured. After a lightning march north, Harold's army destroyed the invaders at Stamford Bridge. Having defeated one invasion, Harold then marched his weary army south for its fateful encounter with the Normans at Hastings.

And now, back to the present and on to Coppergate. Turning left on arrival, the most picturesque buildings are the Three Tuns public house, from the 16th century, and its 19th-century neighbour, once the Yorkshireman pub but now a shop. Further along we turn left into Clifford Street and find the York Dungeon Museum. This displays the grisly fate to which criminals and suspects were subjected in the 'good old days'.

A short walk down Cumberland Street brings us to Cumberland House, built c.1710 and occupied by the Duke of Cumberland on his victorious return from the battle of Culloden in 1746.

Davy Tower

We can now either amble along the south esplanade, or visit the Friargate Wax Museum in Lower Friargate, and then the Museum of Automata, opposite Clifford's Tower in Tower Street. Either way we arrive back at the esplanade, passing as we do so the Davy Tower. This looks remarkably like a house, the only give-away being the stone base. The original tower marked the riverside boundary of the Franciscan Friary, whose land followed the river frontage as far as the Ouse Bridge. The house excluding stone portion, was built in the 1830 s, but the boundary walls of the Friary can still be seen heading towards Tower Street in one direction, and along the river in the other. The stonework portion of the house is all that remains of the 14th. century Davy Tower, and as you see, it still retains an original buttress.

A short walk through the park brings us to the Skeldergate Bridge, and with it our access to Area K.

Area K

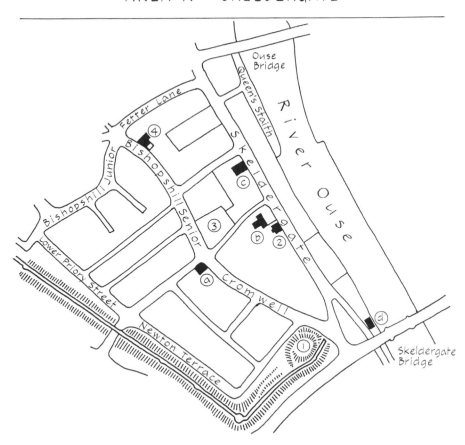

1. Baile Hill
2. 56 Skeldergate
3. Site of St Mary, Bishopshill Senior
4. Bishopshill House

a. Golden Ball
b. Lady Anne Middleton's Hotel
c. Cock and Bottle
d. The Bonding Warehouse

eeping to the riverside we walk through the park to the very attractive and graceful Skeldergate Bridge, a combination of stone and cast iron designed by Thomas Page and completed in 1881. He was also responsible for the design of the Lendal Bridge mentioned in Area A.

Areas K and L, south-west of the Ouse, were populated as far back as Neolithic (the final period of the Stone Age) times, judging by the large number of finds from this area. The oldest thing that we see today, though, is the Old Baile, the motte, or mound, which William the Conqueror had built as part of a motte-and-bailey castle between 1068 and 1069. The castle, of timber, was destroyed by the Danes later that year but was rebuilt by William soon afterwards. So, as we see, the Viking raids were not over yet. Ironically, William himself, being Duke of Normandy, was of Viking descent, that part of northern France having been conquered by Danish Vikings in the late 9th century. It became a duchy under Rollo in 912. William, having invaded and conquered England in 1066, was determined to put down ruthlessly any further Danish attacks. Hence his terrible campaign in Yorkshire in 1069-70, 'the Harrying of the North', in which many perished amid utter devastastion. As calculated, his strong-arm tactics had the desired effect.

The mound is now occupied by a plentiful number of trees, descendants of those first planted between 1722-26. The first stone tower we come to, adjacent to the mound, was built in 1878 following the removal of a section of the wall which had extended down to the Ouse. This part of the wall had incorporated the Skeldergate postern. The wall skirting the mound, though, was built between 1340 and 1370. It is tempting to climb the steps for a walk along the top, and, if you haven't already done the complete circuit of the walls, we can only say that it is a must.

However, for our tour, we leave the mound and head off along Skeldergate, an ancient thoroughfare first mentioned in the 12th century, and which has been extensively redeveloped.

Lady Middleton's Hotel

Area L

a. Scruffy Murphys
b. The Phalanx and Firkin
c. The Nag's Head
d. The Falcon Inn
e. The Ackhorne Inn
f. Walkers Bar
g. Railway King Hotel
h. The Crown Hotel
i. The Other Tap and Spile
j. The Viking Hotel
k. The Corner Pin
l. McMillans Café Bar
m. The Brewer's Arms
n. Lendal Bridge Inn

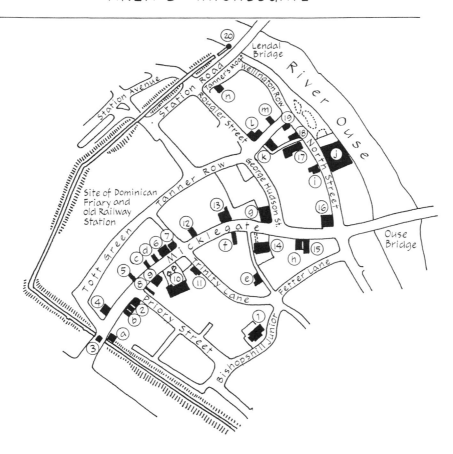

1. St Mary, Bishopshill Junior
2. 99-109 Micklegate
3. Micklegate Bar
4. 142-146 Micklegate - 17th c
5. 113 Micklegate - 16th c
6. Micklegate House
7. Bathurst House
8. 95 Micklegate - 16/17th c
9. 85-89 Micklegate - late 15th c.
10. Holy Trinity church
11. Jacob's Well
12. 70-72 Micklegate - 15/16th c.
13. Garforth House
14. St Martin - cum - Gregory
15. 19 Micklegate - late 15th c.
16. St John the Evangelist
17. All Saints North Street
18. Church Cottages - 15th c.
19. 1 Tanner Row/39 North St.
20 Barker Tower

Leaving Bishopshill Senior, we now find ourselves at a crossroads. To our right is Fetter Lane with not much of interest. Straight ahead lies St Martin's Lane, a very narrow cobbled thoroughfare with origins in the 13th century, but now containing Victorian brick warehouses of two and three storeys, and very atmospheric. Next is Trinity Lane, with a glimpse of the Ackhorne Inn and a building at the far end which we shall visit later on, but our route lies sharp left along Bishopshill Junior. On our right is St Mary's church. The section of the tower below the stone band is a mixture of large and small stones, some laid in herring-bone pattern. This is quite ancient, 10th-century in fact. The upper section, with Norman-style belfry windows, was probably built in the latter part of the 11th century, soon after the Conquest. The parapet was added in the 15th century. The Normans rebuilt the body of the church in the late 11th century, probably at the same time as extending the tower. From then on, the usual alterations and additions began, the biggest in the 13th century, when the chancel was added. The north chapel and south aisle followed a century later. The two windows on the south face of the south aisle are Victorian, as is the porch. Because of the alterations over the centuries it is interesting to see the different types of stonework as one walks around the building. Some very ordered, as in the south aisle, and some random, but with precise work where patching-up has taken place. The remains of a 4th-century house have been recorded in the north-west part of the churchyard.

We now carry on along Bishopshill Junior, and turn right into Priory Street, known in the 18th century as Love Lane (a different connotation entirely). The new name derives from the Holy Trinity Priory whose lands once occupied the whole area. One can only conjecture as to the origins of the previous name. At the end of the street we turn left into Micklegate, with, on the corner, numbers 99-109. These were originally built as a row of two-storey timber-framed and jettied tenements dating from the early 14th century, but they have been considerably altered in the intervening centuries.

St Mary, Bishopshill Junior

Micklegate Bar, the entrance to the City from the west from time immemorial, is sited only 40 metres or so from the equivalent Roman access point. The Bar was the welcoming place for monarchs visiting the City. Richard III, as Duke of Gloucester, came in 1482 and again in the following year as King. His supplanter, Henry VII, came in 1486. His son, Henry VIII, was meant to come this way, but was diverted to Walmgate as the preparations at Micklegate had not been completed. Charles I was greeted here in 1639, only three years before the outbreak of the Civil War. We should also mention that, in our own times, the tradition was maintained for the visit of Queen Elizabeth II in 1972. These welcoming ceremonies were the bright side; the dark side was that the Bar was used for displaying the heads of rebels. One such was Sir Henry Percy (1364-1403) otherwise known as Hotspur, who led a rebellion against Henry IV. Another was Richard, 3rd Duke of York (1411-60), who had attempted to wrest the throne from the Lancastrian Henry VI. In 1745, the heads of some of the leading Jacobite rebels were displayed following the attempt by Charles Edward Stuart, the Young Pretender, to overthrow the Hanoverian monarchy. The Stuarts had reigned in Scotland since 1371, and in England from 1603 until 1714 (that is from James I to Queen Anne). Interestingly, the last Stuart of royal descent was Henry, Cardinal of York, who died in 1807.

But now back to Micklegate Bar itself. It was built in the 12th century reusing Roman gritstone material, which still forms the core of the gate at ground-floor level on the outer side. The façade we see from Micklegate was built in 1827, as evidenced by the strict geometry of both stonework coursing and windows. The structure outside the City Wall, including the turrets, dates from the 14th century. Although the barbican was unfortunately demolished in 1826 (a popular activity at this time as the one at Monk Bar went in 1825 and Bootham in 1831), the Bar as a defensive structure still looks very impressive, and a particularly good view can be had as you approach it along the City Wall. It also houses a small, interesting museum.

Micklegate Bar

We now turn back to walk along Micklegate. You will see that we have highlighted particular buildings on the map either because of their age or their architectural interest, although, we are sure you will agree, the whole street is very attractive. However, we will pick out one or two particular buildings, starting with numbers 88-90 on our left, Micklegate House. This is an imposing brick-fronted house with three storeys and a basement. It has stone quoins to the corners and stone keystones in the voussoirs over the windows. In this respect it is rather reminiscent of Peasholme House in St Saviour's Place, mentioned in Area H. Micklegate House was attributed to John Carr, having been built for John Bourchier. As the plaque on the building notes, his ancestor was Sir John Bourchier, one of the signatories to the warrant for the execution of King Charles I. Peasholme House was also completed in 1752, but the two buildings are different in that one is terraced and the other detached.

On the other side of the road we see a three-storey timber-framed and jettied row of the late 15th century. As usual, shops now occupy the ground floor and the render has been removed to expose the timber framing above. Next door but one is the church of the Holy Trinity which is all that is left of the lands of the former Priory which once stretched from Bishopshill Junior to Trinity Lane. The only parts of the Priory building that remain are the church tower and nave. In fact the Priory was almost twice as long as the present church, with transepts mirrored around the present chancel. Most of the present church was rebuilt in the 19th century.

Round the corner, in Trinity Lane, we see on our right a small but charming cottage on two floors, the first jettied and timber-framed. The building, from the early 16th century, is known as Jacob's Well. Looking at the building now, it is hard to imagine that until recently it had a brick façade to the attic roof space above the first floor, a tribute to the skill of the renovators. The eye-catching carved timber canopy supports by the doorway were once part of the Old Wheatsheaf Inn in Davygate, which was demolished before the turn of the century.

Jacob's Well

Back in Micklegate, on our left, Garforth House is yet another building attributed to John Carr. The façade treatment certainly seems to exhibit the hallmarks of his designs, and the date is right too, i.e. the late 1750 s. Further along on the right is the parish church of St Martin-cum-Gregory. This had modest beginnings, the original 11th-century church only occupying the area of the present nave. Over the course of the next four centuries it gradually grew to the size we see today, and having attained this, narrowly escaped demolition in 1548. The tower was rebuilt in the early 15th century and refaced in brick in 1677. Inside, the 18th-century reredos is very impressive.

Next on our left is George Hudson Street, formerly Railway Street. In a way, the two names are synonymous. George Hudson was born in 1800 at Howsham near York. He was apprenticed as a draper at the firm of Bell and Nicholson. This soon became Nicholson and Hudson. His entrepreneurial skills received a sudden boost when he invested a very large bequest in North Midland Railway shares. In 1837 he became Lord Mayor of York, at a time when he was also manager and founder of the York Banking Company. In the same year he became chairman of the York and North Midland Railway Company, and it was this company that provided the link between York and the West Riding in 1839. This was followed by further extensions to the railway network to Edinburgh via Derby and Newcastle. By 1842 he had become chairman of the Midland Railway Company and an extremely wealthy man. Three years later, a thousand miles of track had been completed, thus justifying his nickname of the 'Railway King'. In August 1845 he was elected Conservative M.P. for Sunderland, being at the time chairman of the Sunderland Dock Company. When the Newcastle and Berwick Railway Company combined with the Newcastle and North Shields, he acquired almost 10,000 shares representing about £145,000. By 1848 the depreciation in railway shares of the leading companies had become so alarming that rigorous investigations were undertaken. In the following year Hudson was forced to resign the chairmanship of the various companies under his control. His debts were found to be enormous, and years of litigation followed.

For twenty years he was involved in a chancery suit with the North Eastern Railway Company. He died in 1871. He was a larger-than-life character whose enterprise established York as the railway city. A century after his death this was recognized by the renaming of the street that we pass on our way to the end of Micklegate.

At the corner with North Street, we come to the Arts Centre, a building that looks suspiciously like a church. In fact it once was a church, that of St John the Evangelist. The south wall is 15th-century, with finely carved stone windows and delicate pinnacles over the mid-19th century buttresses. The east gabled wall is also mid-19th century, and the reproduction windows are good copies of their older counterparts. The lower section of the tower is the oldest part, dating from the 12th century, with the upper portion, of brick and timber, built in 1646.

Continuing along North Street we arrive at another church on our left, that of All Saints. This forms part of a very pleasant little ancient enclave, something of a relief after the rather uninteresting trek along North Street. As with most of York's churches dating from just before or after the Conquest, this also had modest beginnings, in this case in the 12th century. It reached its present size in the 15th century, but started as a cruciform based around the present nave and chancel. It was originally built as the Priory of the Holy Trinity, with land extending as far as the Lendal Bridge. The tower and spire combined appear both tall and slender (only 3 metres square but 37 high) and look slightly at odds with the modest scale of the rest. They were added in the 15th century.

Next door we see a 14th-century row of cottages, retaining their unmistakable character despite the large modern ground-floor window and other modern doors and windows. It forms part of a little cluster of ancient buildings enclosed by Tanner Row and All Saints Lane, and whilst enjoying a tour round the block, we can recommend a visit to the Corner Pin pub for a well-earned refreshment stop.

After this, we can amble through the gardens adjacent to the river on our way to the Lendal Bridge and thus back to were we started our tour of the City. There are a couple of places to mention, though, before we finish. Firstly the site occupied by the old station, and finally the Barker Tower adjacent to the Lendal Bridge.

The site of the old station has served a variety of functions over the centuries. In Roman times it was occupied by baths, serving the city west of the Ouse. In 1227, Henry III granted the land to the Dominican Friars. They remained until the Dissolution and surrendered it in 1538. The land was then sold by the Crown, and for a couple of centuries was used as a nursery garden before being bought by the Trustees of the York and North Midland Railway in 1839. So, from being an open and verdant space for 1,400 years, all was to change dramatically with the onslaught of the new industrial age. The station, planned by George Stephenson with architect G.T. Andrews, was opened on the 4th January 1841 and extended in 1845 to accommodate a new line to Scarborough. The Station Hotel, opened in 1853 and also designed by Andrews, can still be seen at the end of the 'tracks.' The old station was demolished in 1966. The present station was completed in 1877 and designed by Thomas Prosser. To visit the Railway Museum, follow the signs along the Leeman Road just north of the station.

And now to our last port of call, the Barker Tower, cut off from the footpath when the river rises. This round tower of modest height was built in the early 14th century to form the riverside postern at the end of the City Wall. At one time it could also be used, in conjunction with the Lendal Tower opposite, to stretch a chain across the river to bar shipping should the need arise. Its normal everyday role over the centuries was as a base for ferrymen. This activity came to an end when the Lendal Bridge was completed in 1863. Presumably, lengthy discussions then took place as to what its next function should be. We say lengthy because it was not until 1879 that the decision was taken to use it as a mortuary. Thankfully it is not used as such today.

Barker Tower

Incidentally, in case you haven't already had a walk around the City walls, this is a good opportunity to do so by ascending the adjacent steps.

In conclusion, we can only hope that you, like us, have enjoyed the exploration of this great city, which has so much to offer and of which our book has only scratched the surface. Our only regret is that the famous ghosts seem to have disappeared when they saw us coming, so unfortunately we haven't been able to describe any of them. Perhaps you have had better luck.

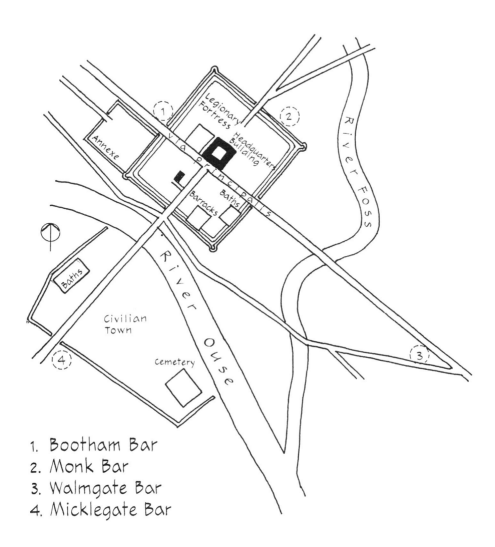

1. Bootham Bar
2. Monk Bar
3. Walmgate Bar
4. Micklegate Bar

Eboracum

List of Churches

		Area
All Saints, North Street	12th C	L
All Saints, Pavement	14th C	F
Bedern Chapel	13th C	C
Centenary Methodist Chapel	19th C	H
Former Ebenezer Primitive Methodist Chapel	19th C	D
Former Wesleyan Chapel	18th C	H
Holy Trinity, Goodramgate	12th C	C
Holy Trinity, Micklegate	11th C	L
St Crux Parish Room, site of St Crux	15th/19th C	G
St Cuthbert, Peasholme Green	11th C	H
St Denys, Walmgate	13th C	I
St George (Catholic Church)	19th C	I
St George, site of		I
St John the Evangelist (Arts Centre)	12th C	L
St Helen	14th C	D
St Margaret, Walmgate	12th C	I
St Martin, Coney Street	12th C	E
St Martin-cum-Gregory	11th C	L
St Mary's Abbey, remains of	11th C	A
St Mary, Bishopshill Junior	10th C	L
St Mary, Bishopshill Senior, site of		K
St Mary's Chapel	15th C	A
St Mary, Castlegate (The York Story)	11th C	J
St Michael-le-Belfrey	16th C	B
St Michael (Spurriergate Centre)	12th C	F
St Olave, Marygate	15th C	A
St Sampson	19th C	G
St Saviour	15th C	H
Unitarian Chapel, St Saviourgate	17th C	H

Index

Further Reading

The Buildings of England,
York and the East Riding.
Nikolaus Pevsner
Penguin Books 1992

Royal Commission on Historical Monuments
City of York Volumes I - V

Ordnance Survey Historical Maps and Guides
Roman and Anglian York
Viking and Medieval York

A Walk around the Snickelways of York
Mark W. Jones

In and Around York
Unichrome (Bath) Ltd. 1991

A History of Yorkshire
The City of York. Edited by P.M. Tillot
Published for the Institute of Historical Research
by the Oxford University Press 1961